A Fancier's Guide to the

NETHERLAND DWARF

by
PHIL BIRCH

Copyright 1997 by
Coney Publications
Chattisham, Ipswich, Suffolk IP8 3QE

ISBN 1-898015-00-7

Set in 11/15 pt Baskerville,
printed and bound in Great Britain
by K.D.S.,
Ipswich, Suffolk.

Introduction

It is a pleasure to write a few words for this book, which is mainly aimed at the new owner and breeder of Netherland Dwarf rabbits, but of course also the established fancier may find it an interesting book to read.

Phil Birch has owned and bred Dwarfs for many years He first joined the National Dwarf Rabbit Club about twenty years ago, has been Chairman of one of the Area Circles, also a committee member, and is still a National judge for the Dwarf rabbit. So he is an ideal person to write this book.

To have something published which is only about this particular breed of rabbit is long overdue. It is many years since the last one was printed.

It covers all aspects of the Netherland Dwarf rabbit from purchasing your first Dwarf, to Housing, Breeding, colours and showing, so even if you only start with a pet it may encourage the pet owner to become a true fancier and eventually start to show them, as this is a great and most enjoyable hobby to be a member of.

I wish Phil and everyone who reads this book all the very best and hope you enjoy reading this publication.

Margorie

Margorie Norbury

President,
National Netherland Dwarf Rabbit Club

PREFACE

I was astonished and exceptionally pleased when the Editor informed me that *Fur & Feather* magazine would like to publish a book based on the series of articles that I wrote for her on the Netherland Dwarf.

From the outset my objective has always been to help the beginner in a practical way to build a stud of Dwarf Rabbits.

The breeding of Dwarfs will always be a difficult challenge, especially where the exhibition rabbit is concerned. In fact it has provided me with the most interest in all my years of involvement in breeding livestock.

I would like to thank my wife for typing my terrible, scrawly writing. She has, frequently, had to come down to my birdroom or rabbit shed to ask what a certain word says.

Also, I would thank Pat and the staff of *Fur & Feather*'s book company *Coney Publications* for all their efforts in publishing my book.

Thank you, also, to the National Netherland Dwarf Club for their support.

P J Birch   October 1997

The author judging a strong Dwarf class at the North East Championship Show

Acknowledgements

Grateful thanks are extended to the following for allowing use of the photographs used in this book:
Michael Byrne; *Fur & Feather*; Simon Beynon; Angela Saunders, Andrew Benson (New Zealand) and Margaret Edwards for providing illustrations.

Contents

First Steps to Understanding the Netherland Dwarf

Joining a Netherland Dwarf Club is a very good way of learning about this popular fancy breed and will enable the newcomer to get in touch with its members, through yearbooks and newsletters, and information stands at leading shows.

The National Netherland Dwarf Rabbit Club (stand photographed above, at the 1996 Bradford Championship Show, manned by Secretary Jean Evans) welcomes membership and will be glad to assist newcomers with their queries.

There are also a number of regional Dwarf clubs and news of their activities, plus advertisements for all their BRC star shows, are advertised in the fanciers' magazine *Fur & Feather*.

CHAPTER 1

Obtaining Stock; Starting to Build a Stud

WHETHER OR NOT YOU ARE A NEWCOMER to the
Netherland Dwarf fancy the biggest problem experienced at the
beginning will be obtaining good foundation stock.

The term "foundation stock" means simply what it says. It is the
nucleus of dwarfs required to build a stud. This can be likened to
building a house: if the foundation is poor the building will crumble
and fall.

Starting with dwarfs can be quite frustrating as there is so much to
take into consideration at the onset. The first thing some prospective
fanciers do wrong is to jump in feet first and buy any stock available. It
is much better to learn a little about the Fancy first, as much as time
and patience will allow. A lot of patience will be needed!

Attend as many stock shows as possible and introduce yourself to
other fanciers, they love talking about their hobby. Be a good listener,
ask questions and show an interest in their stock. Try stewarding, this
way exhibits can be observed more closely. Do not be afraid to ask the
judges questions, the majority will welcome them and be helpful.

At most stock shows you will meet what I call "breeder exhibitors".
These are the people to eventually purchase stock from.

There are a variety of colours of Dwarf to choose so decide which
one you prefer. My advice is to concentrate on one colour at the
beginning. Most Dwarf fanciers will be able to advise as to the name
of a reputable "breeder exhibitor" of your chosen colour. These
exhibitors are the ones most likely to supply the best possible foundation
stock. It is best to approach breeders who keep small studs as they
breed to a limited number of hutches and so are forced to sell stock
regularly to make room for youngsters coming up.

Certain times of the year are better than others for obtaining stock.
The breeders will have bred for particular stock shows and have a glut
of youngsters to rear. Make yourself known to these breeders and ask
if it would be possible to visit their stud. Most breeders will be pleased
to show their stud and champions to interested visitors. It will be an
opportunity to observe the sires and grandsires etc. of your possible

future stock, also to ask any relevant questions.

If stock is available the best start would be to purchase a young adult buck and two does from the same line or family. If the cost of a trio is too expensive consider two does which could possibly be mated. Sometimes to let the breeder have the pick of the resulting litters could secure a deal. If the price is right offer a fee for any future matings you may require and be guided by the breeder. If a good friendship is formed with the breeder it would help in the future.

If you are keen to exhibit it may be possible to purchase a young buck for immediate showing. It is a good feeling when the rabbit wins and the breeder is pleased when he receives recognition for having bred the stock.

If everything goes well, the foundation stock will slowly expand in numbers. Next is to establish the stud by mating young does in the first generation from your purchased stock, to bucks kept by the original breeder. This is the time to learn selection. It is best to be guided by the breeder but gaining personal ideas as well.

In the next generation it may be possible to formulate a personal breeding plan. By this time enough knowledge should have been acquired and hopefully a good enough buck will have been bred from your stock to head your programme. At this stage a stud should have begun to form; this could be possible in the first two years depending on the quality of the initial stock.

If a small stud is kept good fertility is needed as it is better to breed a lot of youngsters from a few dwarfs than a few from a lot. Good mothers and breeders breed the same type of mother. The ideal stud buck is a balanced all round exhibit and is more likely to throw a larger percentage of show type dwarfs. If your buck is lacking in a certain feature it can still be possible to progress. It is a much harder task and should only be used short term. The way to improve from this is to use the cross matching method, i.e. put a doe to the buck which excels in the feature the buck lacks. A doe from this mating needs to be taken back to the original breeder. This doe should be put back to a buck that excels in the feature lacking in the first buck. Hopefully a better buck will appear from this mating to replace the original stud buck as head of your stud. By regularly repeating this method a chance of FIXING the desired type in your stock will occur. When a good buck heads the stud more good bucks should follow in the next generations.

When there are three or four good bucks in a stud and possible replacements being bred a good stud has been formed.

Never be afraid of going to the original breeder for a mating. This is what I call a "distant outcross" and sometimes it generates a new lease of life and offers better prospects to the stud.

Also, give the original breeder access to your stud if he requires it. This is a good way to improve and obtain good quality dwarfs.

A time will come when, hopefully, fanciers will in turn ask for stock from your stud and you can pass on your knowledge and good stock to the prospective fancier.

CHAPTER 2

Colours in the Dwarf

THE CHOICE of colour for the new breeder to take up can be very difficult.

The main reason is because there is such a fine array of colours from which to choose.

Since the Netherland Dwarf standard was altered to accept all colours 'as long as they conform to the normal pattern of accepted colours of other breeds' the list has become endless.

I know I digress, but I have often wondered why more breeders of other varieties do not try to breed the Dwarf equivalent. After all, we have a lot of expert rabbit breeders in the U.K. who could rise to this challenge. Food for thought?

For the new breeder, it is best to stick to the standard accepted colours, especially while learning the trade, so to speak.

The DWARF colours are placed in five groups. (1) Self. (2) Shaded. (3) Agouti Pattern. (4) Tan Pattern. (5) Other Varieties.

Before going through the colours, it is important to say that over the years a lot of problems have occurred in colour breeding Dwarfs, the main one being in mixing any two colours together and then crossing one's fingers. What happens is that true colours are lost, and if this is repeated over a few generations the colours involved become poor in quality and difficult to improve.

Certain colours work well together, however, and if blended correctly colour can actually be improved.

For me, a good coloured Dwarf is like the icing on a cake. If everything else is right and balanced, the rabbit should push for top honours at any show.

Having said that, I must remind new breeders that colour only scores fifteen points in the standard, and obviously it would not pay any dividends to become totally obsessed by colour.

There is a lot more to the Dwarf's makeup than colour, but that's another story!

At this point it is important for me to say that I have a very limited knowledge of genetics, just quite a bit of practical experience.

The **SELF** group of colours gives us white, black, blue, brown and lilac. Of these the **Red Eyed White** is one of the most popular, and usually a good colour for the new breeder to start with.

I will steer clear of saying "it is the easiest". When judging a big class of Whites they can vary from fine white to creamy white and sometimes it is possible to see a grey sort of white.

As pure a white as possible is what is required, and it should be white all over, including the bottom of the feet.

The newcomer to the Dwarf fancy who decides to breed white rabbits has got to learn the art of show preparation. Most judges will not tolerate dirty rabbits and a lot of time and money can be wasted on entries.

Obviously there are some rabbits that are naturally dirty and like digging their bedding, etc. It is very difficult to keep these rabbits clean and if it is a good one it is really annoying!

The main thing is to make sure any show rabbit is kept hutch-clean all the time. A minute a day removing soiled bedding can sometimes save a lot of feet marking, etc.

Another problem with R.E.W. is eye colour. A lot of rabbits have poor eye colour. Look for a deep ruby red when purchasing stock. Avoid the pinky dull eye colour.

The **Blue Eyed** has been a difficult colour for a long time. It is a problem to get the type right, and harsh coat always seems to be a handicap. However, on the brighter side imports from Holland seem to be improving this colour, so good stock should be on the increase and readily available.

Black is another difficult colour to breed, but the challenge can be very rewarding. The difficulty is to breed stock that has no brown tinge. The annoying thing with this colour is that even a good coloured black will go brown and rusty at certain times of the year. To get over this it is important to have rabbits coming up all the time at different stages. Unfortunately it is difficult to build up quality stock levels to achieve this.

The **Blue** although difficult is a beautiful colour and has improved in the last few years. **Black** and **Blue** can be carefully mixed together to the benefit of both colours. The main problem with Blues is white hairs and white patches, especially tail and ear roots. It is difficult to eradicate but as with all faults, can be done with careful selective breeding.

The cinderella colours of the Selfs are definitely **Brown** and **Lilacs**. They are both beautiful colours and deserve more attention from Dwarf breeders, especially the more experienced.

The **Browns** seems to be excellent in colour, but type is difficult to get right. The pool of the best type rabbits need widening and from this there could be a general improvement.

Lilacs are very thin on the ground and need some supporters. These can be produced by carefully blending Blue to Brown and then concentrating on Lilac to Lilac at a later stage. Again, imports from Holland could help.

The main problem with the Holland stock is the difference in type, but again this can be rectified with selective breeding and hard work.

It is important with the cinderella colours to increase and improve the gene pool. This can only be done by breeders collectively using only the best type bucks.

The result: improved overall quality of stock and a bit of competition on the showbench.

The shaded and tan pattern sections of the Dwarf colours definitely give us our most popular colours.

Shaded colours can be blended to Tan Pattern colours, provided this is carefully done and a few simple rules are used.

First a little story. Many years ago, after a blazing row with my ex-wife, I stormed out of the house to the local public house. While I was away, my wife in her infinite wisdom decided to re-organise my breeding programme by letting all the rabbits out. The result was quite a few haphazard matings and over a dozen youngsters were produced due to this magical manoeuvre. All the youngsters were sold as pets except for one. This was a little beauty and enjoyed a reasonable show career.

I never used it for breeding and it ended up as a pet for my niece and lived to a ripe old age of ten. I could have sold this rabbit several times over, but refused to do so, because the parentage was not known.

For the beginner there are three lessons to be learned from this unfortunate episode. Firstly, never buy a Dwarf to be used for breeding on FACE VALUE only. Secondly, don't buy a rabbit unless you know what the parents are like. Thirdly and most important, arrange to visit

One of the most outstanding Red Eyed Whites of all time: Moston One Man, exhibited by Mr & Mrs George Evans with numerous best in show wins including National Netherland Dwarf events and the 1997 Bradford Championship Show. Above: showing excellent allround type, the hallmark of what is required. Below best in show at the 1996 Lancs & Cheshire Dwarf Show, posing beside the club's model "ideal."

the breeder of the rabbit and ask to look at parents, grandparents and other relations etc.

Well, that's enough of story time, I will get back to the colours.

The **Siamese Sable** is one of our most popular colours and a good colour for the beginner to start with. All shades from light, medium to dark are permissible on the show table. However, please try to avoid dark to dark matings, as your rabbits just go darker and darker and the lovely shadings are lost. Light to medium matings are best with the occasional dark mating thrown in.

The biggest problem in modern day Siamese Sable dwarfs is the presence of too many white hairs. A big percentage of the white hair problem is caused by indiscriminate crossing of Marten to Siamese.

The beginner is better sticking to pure Siamese bloodlines for a while and then when he or she feels confident enough, try the following:

Martens and Siamese Sables can be carefully mated together providing a very simple rule is used. Never put Siamese bred from a Marten x Siamese mating back to a pure Siamese bloodline. The reason to avoid doing this can be simply explained. The Siamese from the cross will obviously have fifty percent of Marten genes. When put back into the Siamese Sable bloodline, things may be O.K. in the first generation but troubles start later.

What happens is the dominant Marten genes start to appear, but in a different form. Siamese Sables will be bred with white pads, white hairs inside nose. Also, there will be white hairs in ears and the possibility of many white hairs over the entire body.

These faults will take years to eradicate and could possibly ruin a good stud of Siamese Sables.

If it was a buck that was used from the cross, the problems will probably be worse. The simple reason for this is that over say a twelve month breeding programme, the buck will breed a lot more youngsters than a doe would have done. Obviously the above faults will appear in more rabbits quicker. This is one of the reasons why a doe should always be used for outcrossing, to improve any particular feature of the Dwarf. This will be dealt with in a later chapter.

An extension of the Marten x Siamese rule is "Only use Siamese from a Marten/Siamese cross for Marten breeding". These rules remind me of another little story.

A very old fancier friend of mine, sadly no longer with us, used to have a brilliant saying. Whilst in the 'Chair' in discussions with fellow fanciers and passing on endless information, he would say: 'Please remember the Golden rules'. Somebody among the people present would always say: 'What Golden Rules?' With bellowing laughter my old friend would retort: 'There are no Golden Rules when breeding livestock'. While I go along with this up to a point, I am of the opinion that if you have made practical mistakes once, why do it again. What I have said above are simply ways of avoiding ruining a good stud of Dwarfs.

A good example of a Seal Point Dwarf, one of the more difficult colours to perfect

One of my own favourite colours of Dwarf is the Smoke Pearl. However, it is a rather difficult colour for the beginner breeder. In fact it is sometimes difficult for established breeders. Where in the Siamese Sables all shades are permissible on the show bench, only one colour or shade of smoke is acceptable. The standard calls for the saddle to be smoke in colour, shading to a pearl grey beige on flanks.

For the beginner this is difficult to visualise. What I like to see is a pinky dove tinge on the smoke colour. It is much better to actually look at a good coloured Smoke than to visualise something that is written. Please try to look at a good coloured Smoke, so that you know what is required.

The main problem you will come across when breeding Smokes, is that there is a tendency for the saddle colour to gradually go darker or bluey. If this fault is not corrected, eventually a bigger percentage of your breeding stock will acquire this fault. It is similar to the dark shade that happens in the Sable.

This, in my opinion, is where the answer lies to correct the fault and achieve balance of colour in the stud. If you cannot rectify the fault by using a very light coloured smoke, no harm can be done by trying the following:

Always use a dark smoke or bluey doe for this breeding venture. I would very rarely use a dark Smoke buck, unless it really excelled in every other department. Even then I would only use it in a very limited way. It would have to improve or maintain good type or it would not be used. The dark Smoke doe is by far the better option.

Take this rabbit to as good a light shade coloured Siamese Sable buck you can find. The Smoke does out of this cross, if good colour, should be bred to your best coloured Siamese Smoke buck. The next generation **should** see a bigger percentage of correct coloured Smokes being bred. Light coloured Siamese Sable does bred from the Smoke/ Sable cross could still be useful if the first attempt fails. These should be taken back to the good coloured Siamese Smoke buck. This is what I call dipping Sable, but it should not be done too often. The reason being that if you are concentrating on a stud of Smokes, if done too often you will get overrun with Siamese Sables.

Any rabbits bred that are not required for future breeding, please let them go for pets. We are lucky to have a breed that is usually always in demand by the pet trade. This being so there is no excuse for misfit dwarfs being ferried round the Dwarf fancy as so-called breeding stock. This is the case with all colours of Dwarf rabbits.

However, there is always a possibility of giving other breeders the opportunity of either buying or having access to the better quality dwarfs that you no longer require. This is where the Dwarf fancy fails

A young Siamese Sable doe. She just needs to fill out all round to make an excellent adult. Note lovely body shape.

at present. We have got to help each other more. The fancier specialising in certain colours may require rabbits you do not want. If you provide him with parentage and how the Dwarf was bred, everything is O.K. If this was done on a wider basis, all colours would gradually improve and a better quality of dwarf would appear in bigger numbers on the showbench.

I have known breeders in the past to use R.E.W. to improve the Siamese Smoke in colour. This is not an option I have used, but I suppose on an experimental basis only, could be worth a try. The main problems I can see with this are white hairs and white toe nails appearing in the stock.

We will always have the presence of white hairs in coloured rabbits. However, as long as there are faults in the Dwarf standard, we should try to keep them to a minimum or eradicate them altogether. This will always be a challenge for the coloured Dwarf breeder.

A way forward is to try to avoid breeding rabbits together with white hairs in the same place. An example of this would be a rabbit with a few white hairs in the ears. This should be bred to a rabbit with no white hairs in the ears. This may sound so simple and logical but you would be surprised how often it is overlooked.

The last of the colours and definitely the Cinderella colours are the **Seal Point** and **Tortoiseshell.** These are still shaded rabbits and this should always be remembered.

First, the Tortoiseshell, a lovely colour, but not very popular in the Dwarf fancy. When they are seen in any numbers, usually at stock shows or at our largest open championship show, there is usually a wide range of shades. There are not enough with the rich orange saddle. This is what we are really looking for, together with gradual shadings to blue black on flanks.

The biggest problems I can see are some rabbits are a wishy washy colour with both orange and blue-back running into each other. Secondly, we have rabbits at the other end of the scale which are too dark and show no orange or hardly any at all. What we are after is a midpoint between the two and yet, it is very difficult.

Perhaps a lesson or two could be learned from the Dwarf Lop fancy. It is one of their most popular colours. I have a limited practical experience of breeding Dwarf Lops in this colour and orange/fawn and black was used. Both are the right ground colours, so perhaps dipping orange or dipping black could work. Use Netherland Dwarfs, of course.

Personally, I would first form a backbone of Tort to Tort bred rabbits and use the above gradually and carefully. What the colour wants is more fanciers to have a go. Definitely a challenge for any person who is prepared to give it a try. One thing for sure is that a lot of pet rabbits would be bred. I suppose it would help to pay the feed bill.

Finally the **Seal Point**. This colour is a dilute colour to the Siamese Sable. It is not very popular and it is a difficult colour to breed. This however, takes nothing away from its beauty as in Siamese Sable. We get light, medium and dark turning up in the breeding pen. Unfortunately, the standard as with the Siamese Smoke gives us just one colour. This is the medium colour, which the standard states as 'rich dark sepia brown on ears, nose, feet and tail, shading to a lighter colour on body'. What I have said earlier about breeding the Siamese Smoke can be useful in breeding the Seal Point.

The difference being that Siamese Sable should not be used very often. The reason for this is that the Seal Point is such a dilute colour that the dominant genes of the Siamese Sable will breed too many dark coloured rabbits. This is where the use of a light coloured Seal Point buck could be useful. Strictly for breeding of course.

In a lot of colours of Dwarfs, especially where specialisation is taking place, there will be dwarfs in the stud which will have no place on the showbench. This is all well and good providing enough rabbits are being bred percentage wise, which are a good enough colour for show purposes.

If this is not happening in your stud, records need to be looked at and probably a breeding programme set out to rectify this. The problem with what I call the Cinderella colours is that it is very difficult to fix the required type on good coloured stock.

In these colours there is a shortage of pre-potent bucks and to a lesser extent, there is a limited number of rabbits carrying the dwarf gene. If this situation could be improved upon, these colours would produce better quality dwarfs in the future.

Without doubt the **Tan Pattern** section of Dwarf colours, just like the shaded, provides us with some of the more popular colours.

For the beginner breeder they are a little more difficult, because pattern markings are required in addition to the ground colour.

The first two colours I describe have a shaded ground colour; the rest have a self ground colour.

Marten Sable

The Marten Sable is one of the most popular colours in modern day Dwarfs. As well as being popular, there are some very good quality Martens around at present. The owners of some of these rabbits are comparative newcomers and are doing really well. This is proof that the beginner, provided good stock can be purchased, can do well almost straight away.

I will always have a soft spot for the Marten, having bred them for many years. They have given me lots of pleasure and it has been good to see the colour climb from humble beginnings to its present status.

As with the Siamese Sable, the shaded body colour is accepted on the show bench in all shades from light, medium to dark.

Obviously what has been said earlier about dark to dark matings, applies just as much to Martens as it does to Siamese.

What gives the Marten Sable its added beauty is definitely its pattern markings. The marking colour should be as pure white as possible. This includes eye circles, inside of ears, line of jaws, inside of nose, belly and underside of tail.

In addition to this the chest, flanks, rump and feet should be well ticked with longer white hairs. This is known as 'ticking' and should not be confused with the normal white hairs that are sometimes found in the coloured area, outside the white pattern as explained above.

There are two main differences between ticking and white hairs.

Ticking is a definite requirement and an added beauty to the white pattern, where white hairs are faults and should be penalised accordingly. Also, ticking is a long guard hair, with a sharp white tip. The more ticking up the flanks the better, especially if it is evenly distributed.

Finally, before I forget, the triangle behind the neck should be as small as possible.

This all may sound difficult to the newcomer. I suggest the best way to progress is to look at a good coloured Marten, so that you can see for yourself just what is required. The sharp contrast between the general body colour and marking colour is very striking on a good coloured Marten.

If the Marten is of good type the contrast between the body colour and markings seems to make the Marten look even better in type. This is especially so round the head area. The eye circles and line of jaw seem to define the head more.

It may be some sort of optical illusion or trick on the eyes, but a good Marten Sable always seems capable of being at or near the top in a good Dwarf challenge class. Obviously this is good for the newcomer, as the efforts you put in initially could give you some early success and therefore keep the interest going.

This is very important in your early years as a colour breeder. It helps to cushion all the disappointments that occur. When you have your mishaps and little setbacks, please take heart in the fact that even the top breeders experience the same problems. The difference is that

A very sound Marten Sable Dwarf showing good pattern, which tends to enhance the overall type

the established breeder has learned how to cope and contain the problems.

It is very important to progress nice and steady at the beginning, thereby gradually learning more as you go along. You will recall in my first chapter I mentioned specialising in one colour, and this is a good way to start off. However, there are definite ways to progress further, as the interest grows.

The following is just an example. Suppose you have got going with Siamese Sables, and you really fancy the Martens? One good way, if there is a budget problem, is of course, the Marten-Siamese cross, described earlier.

If the cross is used carefully and the simple rules are observed, there is no reason why a useful stud of Martens could not be built up. This could be done steadily and at a comparatively low cost. For example, you could arrange a mating to a top class Marten with your best Siamese doe. This could put you on your way.

Providing you keep your Siamese Sable bloodline pure, there is no reason whatsoever why good quality Dwarfs cannot be bred in both colours. The Siamese Sables bred from the cross, if good quality but not required by yourself, could be offered to the breeder who supplied you with the mating. Marten breeders will always make use of a good Siamese doe, as will be found out shortly.

Another way to start is to go for straight Marten breeding and obtaining a trio of Marten to Marten bred stock. The overall quality of Martens is so good at present that this would be the best way to start, although obviously it would cost more.

The biggest problem faced when breeding Martens is white hairs appearing in the wrong place. White hairs that appear in the saddle, on outside of ears and above the nose on the face are faults. When Marten to Marten matings are carried out over many generations, there is a possibility that the Marten genes become over dominant.

Early signs of this are too many white hairs appearing in the saddle. This leads to white hairs in outside ears, and up the face extending from the nose.

Extreme cases result in a putty nose (white spot on nose above nostrils) which is a disqualification. Before this stage has been reached the situation can be rectified by a Marten Siamese cross. In effect this cross redresses the balance and the Martens should gradually become free of the problem.

In some strains where the problem is severe the Marten from the cross may have to be taken back to the Siamese again.

Sometimes the Martens bred from the cross lack the required amount of ticking. This is usually rectified by going back to Marten breeding again.

Really, it is all about finding the right balance. This is difficult to achieve over many generations, but then again nothing is easy when colour breeding.

Marten Smoke

The Marten Smoke is a little more difficult for the beginner. As with the Siamese Smoke, only one colour is permissible on the show bench.

The body colour of the Marten Smoke is exactly the same as the Siamese Smoke. In the white pattern on the Marten Smoke however, the undercolour on the white belly should be Fawn.

In recent years the Marten Smoke has really improved and this has been down to one or two really dedicated breeders. These people have specialised in the colour and have been totally committed 100% to improving the colour. Also, stock has been made available by these breeders, so other people have reaped the benefits and at the same time the colour has become more popular. Obviously the beginner can take advantage of this situation as good quality stock is usually available.

This success story could be repeated in any of the rarer colours. All that is needed is a nucleus of dedicated breeders, helping each other and using a concentrated gene pool of good stock.

The Importance of Shadings

It is important at this stage to mention shadings. In both colours above, and in all colours in the shaded section, there is a requirement for body shadings. These should gradually blend from saddle to flanks, without any patchiness or blotches, etc.

Sometimes when rabbits are moulting it is inevitable that there could be patchy colour. When the rabbit has finished moulting, however, there should be no patchiness. A patchy rabbit could win at local shows, though, especially if type is good. However, be very careful if you use this rabbit in the breeding pen. Always mate the rabbit to one that excels in colour and shadings. It is so easy for this fault to creep into the rest of the stock, so be careful.

Before leaving the Marten Smokes and Sables, it is possible for the beginner breeder to gradually progress to breeding both types of Sables together. Also eventually both types of Smokes could be built in. There have been a few successful breeders who have done this, but the challenge is enormous. Also, the beginner may fall into the trap of getting to the above set-up too soon. The more colours that are bred, the more time and effort is needed for the hobby.

Unfortunately some people are really bitten by the rabbit bug and this can be their downfall. Building more and more hutches is not the answer to improving your stock. Also, don't forget, the more rabbits you keep, the deeper it bites into your expenses. It also takes up more of your valuable time. The bigger set up requires the keeping of a good record system, and this will be covered in a later chapter.

All in all, it is far better to start in a small way with one colour, and build up gradually.

Most of the successful studs that have been around a long time have done this. Quite a few have changed colours along the way, but usually achieve success sooner or later whatever colour they keep. Their success is usually down to following set patterns of breeding, including inbreeding and outbreeding. Also, they have acquired the ability to select stock, improve their feeding and breeding techniques. Above all, they have become good stockmen and have a good knowledge of the Dwarf rabbit.

These are the breeders that beginners should approach for their first stock. They can be found exhibiting at all the top stock shows and usually winning on a regular basis.

Otter

The Otter is available in the four self ground colours, namely black, blue, chocolate and lilac.

As with the self colours, blacks and blues are the more popular, with chocolate and lilac being very thin on the ground. The reason for this is exactly the same as explained in the Self Section and can be rectified in a similar fashion.

The pattern colour in the Otter is basically a creamy white, as opposed to the pure white in the Marten Sable. On top of this there is a tan border dividing the white and coloured parts. The Tan should also encircle the nostril and go under the chin. Also, there is a requirement for a tan eye circle and small triangle behind the neck. Finally, tan ticking is required on chest, flanks and rump, not forgetting a tan border on the outside and a covering of tan on the inside of the ears.

It is the amount of tan ticking and the depth of tan that really sets this colour off.

The Otter was accepted as a standard colour around 1980. They were bred well before this, however, but they were usually sold as pets.

In the early eighties I built a small stud of Otters. These were produced by a Marten Sable cross Self Black mating. Otter breeders at the time used Agouti cross Marten Sables. Tanning, or the lack of it, was the problem at first, but this was soon improved upon. Present-day Otters are very good and there are some excellent Dwarfs on the

A very good blue Otter showing excellent type proportions with good colour and tanning

show bench. They are popular, and availability of stock is usually good. They are a very good colour for the beginner.

In the early days I noticed that the Otter gene was very dominant and sometimes the present-day Otters suffer from this. A similar situation occurs as explained previously with Marten Sables. The difference is, as well as white being up the nose, face and body parts, a tan brindling occurs. This spoils the colour and the fault needs to be remedied.

A mating to a Self Black is a way of restoring the balance. This works exactly the same as the Marten-Siamese cross mentioned earlier.

Established breeders usually use a Black doe, but the beginner who is learning about the colour could obtain a mating from a Black buck. If budget is limited, this is the cheapest way; there is usually always somebody around who will help a beginner. Please don't let Blacks bred from this cross go back to Black breeders. (They have enough problems without using rabbits that carry the Otter gene!)

Colour breeding in general is all about trying to improve the colours, but at the same time keeping colour blood-lines pure.

Fox

The Fox Dwarf is a beautiful colour, but has never enjoyed the popularity of the Marten Sables or Otters. Obviously it needs more breeders to take it up. There is no reason at all why it should not become as popular as the other tan pattern colours.

As with the Otter, the self ground colours are black, blue, chocolate and lilac. The white pattern is exactly the same as the Marten Sable, explained above. If colour is good the contrast between black and white is very striking.

Obviously if this is combined with very good type, they are a force to be reckoned with in the challenge classes. Progress can be made as the colour is in the hands of a few dedicated breeders.

The Fox boasts the only Supreme Champion in the Netherland Dwarf championship lists. This is a definite sign of its potential.

Tan

The final colour, and to me the saddest in the whole section, is the Tan. This colour is virtually extinct in Dwarfs. This is so sad, especially when you consider the success of its normal counterpart.

Again, the Tan is accepted in the same self ground colours as the Otter and Fox. The pattern colour has obviously to be a rich Tan, and should follow the same pattern marking explained in previous colours.

What a beautiful Dwarf this colour would make! Perhaps the only answer to get the colour going, is by dwarfing the normal Tan down. We have enough expert breeders in both breeds, so surely there is a future for this colour?

The **AGOUTI PATTERN SECTION** of Dwarf colours gives us a varied and interesting collection; three of the colours are dilute, and there is always difficulty maintaining good quality banding. Every colour in this section needs to have banded colour in the make-up of its coat.

When the coat is blown into or parted by the hand, the coat should show the following banding:

Starting from the base of the skin there is the first band, usually known as undercolour, or base colour. Next comes the intermediate band, always in a contrasting colour. The top banding is usually a mixture of colour and ticking, and the outside of the ears are laced with this colour.

Finally, the eye circles, underside of tail and belly colour are white.

Mr J Baldock's Agouti, best in show at the National Netherland Dwarf Club's adult stock show in 1993. This was a very good Agouti giving John an excellent win

This gives a general pattern for all colours in the Agouti section, however there is a slight variation in some colours, so before going through these it is important to stress the need for CLEARLY defined bands. This definition of colour shows the real beauty of the Agouti Pattern. This is a very important requirement for a rabbit to push for top honours at the highest level.

The Agouti is by far the most popular colour in this section, and it is usually a colour the beginner-breeder can do quite well with.

The base colour should be a dark slate blue, with an orange band as the intermediate colour. The top colour is a rich chestnut shade, interspersed with black ticking. Eye circles and underparts are white with a slate base undercolour, and ears should be laced with black.

A big percentage of present-day Agoutis fail in some of the above required features.

The Agouti was one of the first colours in the Dwarf rabbit. In the early days they were very good type and so were mixed with the other colours. Then they were used with different colours to create yet more colours, so credit for this wide range must go to the Agouti.

On the debit side, agoutis bred out of the various colour crosses have been put back to pure Agouti lines. The solid coloured Agouti lines of old, with their rich chestnut top, have not been kept pure enough, and this is why when confronted with a big class of Agoutis, some of our judges start scratching their heads.

It is possible to come across four or five different shades of top colour. Also, undercolour and definition of banding is sometimes very poor.

Usually the excellent typed exhibit can carry some of these faults, but the beauty of the colour has been lost and there is no way this type of exhibit should push for top honours; otherwise they will be used in the breeding pen and colour will never improve.

Having said this, there are still some good Agouti lines in this country. In fact, Agoutis took some of the major honours in recent years and it is a pity that these are not around in numbers.

The beginner should purchase stock from pure Agouti lines. By doing this you will stand a fair chance of competing in the big classes found at stock shows.

Many Agoutis have very pale grey sides and this is very difficult to eradicate.

Never mate two rabbits together which share this fault. Also, two rabbits which both have poor undercolour.

Once you have started with a good foundation stock of Agoutis, keep them pure. If you use an Agouti with another colour, don't put the Agoutis from the cross back into pure Agouti lines.

I have used Agoutis in my Blacks many times, but Agoutis from the crosses have never been sold for Agouti breeding or used in Agouti lines. Again, when buying Agoutis or bringing in an outcross from another stud, find out the parentage. I have covered this before, but it is still very important.

Every time a mating is being considered, ask the question: "Will this improve colour?"

Sometimes the does in the stud carry good colour and the bucks do not. If this is the case and especially if inbreeding has been taking place, get an outcross.

Take your best coloured doe to the best coloured buck you can find, and have her mated. There are a few good coloured bucks around at present, so take advantage of it. Paying a few pounds for a mating to a good coloured buck is better than to keep breeding average coloured Dwarfs. And being selective when trying to improve colour is also very important.

Using a good balance of inbreeding and outbreeding is a sure way of 'fixing' good colour.

The **Opal** is sometimes called the Blue Agouti. It is a dilute colour of the Agouti. The base colour or undercolour is a lighter colour of slate than the Agouti base colour.

The intermediate band is Fawn with the top colour showing a pale shade of blue. Ears are laced with blue. Eye circles, underside of tail and belly are white with a slate undercolour.

Over the years I have bred a few Opals myself from Blue to Agouti matings. When writing about the Tan Pattern section I mentioned Otters being bred by Agouti-Marten Sable matings. These are just two examples of how the Agouti has created other Dwarf colours.

In fact in the Agouti pattern section, the Agouti is probably part of the make-up of all the colours, with the exception of the CHINCHILLA and SQUIRREL.

Back to the Opal. As I have written previously, it is more difficult to get a good definition in the banding, with the dilute colours. Even so, it is a requirement in the standard and should always be given careful consideration when matings are being selected.

In the late seventies and early eighties, a well known Scottish breeder built up an excellent stud of Opals. In fact I made one of these best in section when judging a National stock show; it beat some very good Agoutis on the day, excelling in type and of very good colour. Present-day Opals are not as good as these earlier exhibits.

However, there must be some of the above bloodlines spread around the country. Obviously if some of the established Opal breeders have stock from this bloodline, better quality Opals should eventually start to appear.

The **Lynx** although a very attractive colour is comparatively rare in this country. The standard calls for a white undercolour or base colour. The intermediate band should be bright orange and the top colour is defined as orange shot silver, with the tips of the fur being silver.

Belly, eye circles, inside ears and underside of jowl should be white. Chest should match flanks; blueish tinge and blue undercolour are classed as serious faults.

Dare I stick my neck out and say this is the Lilac Agouti - more about this later.

The Lynx is a very delicate dilute colour and there is always a problem getting the required definition in the banding. The difficulty is getting the orange band defined on the white under colour: because the colour is so dilute, the orange is usually a pale shade and sometimes we get a fawny colour.

Obviously when this happens there is a tendency for the intermediate colour to run into the undercolour. When this occurs the banding is virtually non-existent, and a judge could pass these rabbits on as poor coloured Fawns.

A more important problem for the Lynx is that at present only one or two breeders have the colour. This is a pity as such an attractive colour would be seen more on the show table if only a few more breeders could be encouraged to take it up.

Next is the **Chinchilla**, a sparkling blend of black and white which makes this colour a beauty. The colour standard varies slightly from the other Agouti colours, because it came from the normal Chinchilla

An excellent Chinchilla Dwarf showing superb ear carriage and frontage and set off with sparkling colour. A beautiful example

standard. When you first look at the colour it should resemble the real Chinchilla.

The base colour is a dark slate blue, which should be definitely wider than the intermediate band of pearl. (For the beginner, pearl can be defined as "off white").

Above the pearl band there is a narrow line edging of black. Then there is a definite reminder in the standard that pearling should be clearly defined.

Top colour is grey, ticked with black hairs and this ticking can be either wavy or even. The wavy ticking is known as a mackerel top in Normal Chinchilla circles.

Ears are laced black. Flanks and chest are ticked with a uniform shade of pearl, to be slightly lighter than body. Also, the neck fur is lighter but confined to the nape only. Finally, eye circles are light grey.

I bred Normal Chinchillas for many years, and found it very difficult getting good colour, even with the coat length of one and a quarter inches. So imagine how hard it is to get the colour perfect on the dwarf's approximately half-inch coat length.

However, with all the difficulties there are some good Chin Dwarfs about. The colour has gained a lot of popularity in the last few years. Again, this is down to a few breeders being dedicated enough to improve the colour. The beginner should be able to purchase stock off these breeders and get a good start.

Please don't mix the Chinchilla with the Agouti, there is **no advantage** with this mating whatsoever. The result is very poor coloured Chins, which can't touch the pure bred lines. A good typed Chinchilla with sparkling colour can push in any Dwarf challenge.

If definition can be improved a little more, I can see the colour gaining more popularity still.

The **Squirrel** is another very attractive colour and a direct dilute colour to the Chinchilla. The top colour is a sparkling blend of blue and white, with blue ticking. The intermediate colour is pearly white, with a light slate undercolour. Ears are laced with blue. Eye circles, underside of tail and belly are white, with light slate undercolour.

Again, the greatest difficulty is establishing good definition in the banding. The occasional really good Squirrel turns up on the show table; these are usually rabbits that have been bred out of the prominent Chinchilla lines outlined above.

In fact both colours are compatible with each other and a Squirrel with poor banding can be bred to a Chinchilla with excellent definition, in order to make further improvements.

Most studs of Chinchillas usually breed the occasional Squirrel. These can be successfully blended back into the Chinchilla line again. However, because the Chinchilla is the dominant colour, they will turn up in greater numbers.

To adopt Squirrel to Squirrel matings for many generations could result in wishy washy colour. Although this breeding pattern would result in more Squirrels in the stud, occasional matings to Chinchillas would be required.

So it is all about getting the right balance between the two colours.

Well, that covers the listed colours in the AGOUTI PATTERN section. However, I cannot leave this chapter without mentioning the **Cinnamon.**

I first saw this colour in Satins many years ago and its outstanding beauty really impressed me. The top colour is brown, with a stronger brown ticking, giving an overall brown effect. The intermediate colour is Orange, which should be clearly defined from the light blue undercolour.

The only problem with this colour is that it is so scarce. I know of only one breeder with the colour, but I could be wrong. Perhaps eventually more may become available and the Cinnamon could start to grow in popularity.

The Cinnamon is not a dilute colour so it could be a little easier to breed than say the Opals or Lynx. What I mean by this is that getting good definition in the banding should be easier. Having said this, because the colour is so thin on the ground, building numbers up would be difficult at first. The colour is also known as the Chocolate Agouti, and the Lynx as explained above is a dilute colour to the Cinnamon. This is why I said the Lynx was the Lilac Agouti.

Well, as you can see, all four self colours - black, blue, chocolate and lilac - play their part in the make-up of the agouti pattern colours. When you add these to the Chinchilla and Squirrel, you can see the varied and interesting colour make up of the section.

Himalayan —

THE MOST POPULAR COLOUR in this section, without doubt, is the Himalayan.

Four colours are recognised in the Himalayan variety, namely Black, Blue, Chocolate and Lilac. The pattern colour of the rabbit follows the normal Himalayan, that is as regards to distribution of colour.

The body colour is white, and the nose, ears, front feet, hind feet and tail are to be any of the four colours mentioned above. The nose, usually termed smut, should be well up between the eyes, the bigger the better. All the points (another term for the markings) should be as deeply coloured as possible.

The beauty of this colour is definitely the contrast between the white body and the markings. On a good type rabbit the colour points look particularly striking.

The main problem with this variety is getting a good deep colour on the Points.

In the late seventies/early eighties I had a good stud of Himalayans; I tried all ways to improve the colour further still, but without much success. The biggest mistake I made was using a Siamese Sable cross carelessly. Unfortunately I put Siamese Sables from this cross back into the Sable line again. The reason I did this was because type was very good in the Siamese Sables. All went well in the first generation, but subsequent matings revealed my mistake: very light pads and even white pads started to appear in the Siamese Sables. Also, white hairs appeared in abundance. It took me a few years to rectify these faults so please don't make the same mistake!

If you are forced to use a Siamese Sable on the Him., use a **dark** one. Then only use rabbits from this cross for Himalayan breeding. I often thought of using a Black; however at the time type was not very good in the Blacks that I had.

This brings me to another important point when colour breeding. Don't use another colour to improve a particular colour, unless both rabbits are good type.

If type is lost at the expense of a little improvement in colour, then a lot of time has been wasted.

Going back to the Himalayans, I personally think a cross to a Black could be a useful attempt to improve depth of colour. Obviously, this cross would have to be used on an experimental basis only.

If success did come from the cross, it would then possibly be better to keep to Himalayan to Himalayan matings for quite a few generations.

This is usually always the best way to prosper, but your selection of matings should be very strict.

The Himalayan really comes out in force at the major stock shows. It is not uncommon to see classes of over twenty. I get a lot of personal enjoyment out of judging a big class of Himalayans, they remind me of a regiment of soldiers.

They are a good colour for the beginner to progress into. A lot of pleasure can be derived from seeing youngsters get more colour as they grow older.

Orange

Next comes the Orange. This is a very attractive colour but difficult to get right. The main body colour should be a bright orange and gradually shading down the flanks. The colour needs to go well down the fur, with a white undercolour.

Chest colour should match flanks. The eye circles, inside of ears, underside of jowl and tail, and belly to be white.

A good coloured example of the Himalayan Dwarf bred by Mrs Angela Saunders – probably the best Himalayan stud in the country

Too few people have this colour, and it is not often that you see a very good Orange Dwarf.

One of the main problems seems to be too much black ticking on the body colour. Also ears and face have a tendency to be very light in colour. Obviously the standard doesn't say these are faults, but when compared with the rich orange colour of the rex version, the Dwarf Orange colour looks comparatively poor. Perhaps the Orange has suffered because over the years it has been intermixed with the agouti, too much.

This would definitely explain why there is a lot of black ticking around.

The only way forward I can see, is that concentration should be focused on orange to orange matings.

Again the same old story applies about being really selective when making pairings, in order to further improve colour.

It is also possible to make the occasional cross to the Fawn - more about this later.

By following this advice it could be possible to slowly improve colour.

If the agouti cross was the culprit for creating the black ticking, the further you get away from it the better. However, it could take several generations of careful selective breeding before improvements could be seen.

Fawn

The Fawn is a dilute colour to the Orange. The saddle colour or main body colour should be a warm Fawn, and shading down the flanks.

Again, as with the Orange, colour should go well down the fur, with a white undercolour.

Chest to match flanks, eye circles, inside of ears, underside of tall and jowl and belly to be white.

As can be seen the pattern colour for the Orange and Fawn are very similar.

The term warm Fawn is difficult to explain.

I suggest the beginner should look at a class of Fawn Rex at one of the major shows. This is what the colour should ideally be like. Again, black ticking is a problem with Fawns as well as very light drab colour.

The latter of the two is a little easier to sort out.

A few years ago I bred a few Fawn Rex and adapted the following with a little success.

When the colour in the Fawns was going too light and wishy washy, a mating to an Orange Rex was made. The best coloured Fawns from the cross were put back to Fawns again.

This was repeated, until the correct Fawn colour started to appear. The same should work with Orange and Fawn Dwarfs. Both colours can be blended together carefully, in order to improve each other.

The black ticking is a bigger problem and only patience and perseverance with selective breeding will eradicate this.

Steel

The final colour listed in this section is the Steel.

A bright Steel colour is required throughout. Head, feet, ears and belly to match body colours. Colour to be as free as possible from a brown tinge, undercolour should be a dark slate and carried well down the skin, with no trace of a grey or yellow band. Undercolour of tail can be lighter than the body.

Then there is a list of faults, as follows: Band in undercolour, feet and ears not matching body colour, and barred feet.

Although quite a lengthy list of requirements for the colour, it is still an attractive variety, especially when you see a good one.

Not many breeders have this colour and possibly that's the main problem.

Around the late seventies and early eighties there was an excellent stud of Steels, which came from the Midland area. I once remember one of those Steels taking best of breed from almost one hundred Dwarfs.

Unfortunately, when the breeder gave up the stud got broken up. I have not seen Steels as good as these since. The colour has also been dogged by the occurrence of white tails. This is very difficult to eradicate. I have had plenty of experience with this fault in Blacks.

As with everything else, with a little care and attention to detail these problems can be overcome.

In recent years some very good Steels have been imported from Holland, so there could be some improvement in the near future.

Once these Steel lines are established and a few breeders can get hold of stock, we could be looking at another Dwarf success story.

Well, that covers the listed colours in this section, but the last sentence in the standard adds further interest to the Dwarf's fine array of colours:

"Accept any colour so long as it conforms to the normal pattern of accepted colours of other breeds."

Literally what this means is that any colour of Dwarf can be accepted on the show bench. This of course is provided that the colour is recognised in other breed standards.

When this first came into being, I was personally against it, feeling that we had enough colours already.

In recent years I have changed my mind, and believe it adds a new dimension to breeding coloured Dwarfs.

For anybody that likes to experiment or dabble about, so to speak, the colour varieties are endless.

For example what about an Argente Bleu Netherland Dwarf. Or a Red Dwarf - following the New Zealand Red colour.

These colours would certainly be eye catching, and possibly make a few judges scratch their heads. You can well see why I said referring to colour, there is something for everybody.

We have had the Dutch pattern Netherland Dwarf for quite a while, but they are thin on the ground at present.

However, what about the **English marked Netherland Dwarf**, or E.M.D.'s as they are affectionately known.

The first ones appeared quite a long time ago, bred by a well known Norfolk fancier.

In recent years however there has been a revival and we even have an E.M.D. Circle within the Netherland Dwarf Rabbit Club.

These breeders have taken on a very different challenge. The problem seems to be that only fifty per cent of the rabbits carry the required English markings. Also, the problem of fixing Dwarf type is very difficult.

When you put these two problems together, the chance of breeding an E.M.D. of good enough standard to show becomes enormous.

These few fanciers who belong to the E.M.D. Circle are really trying to do just that.

I have been involved in some of these projects and I heartily wish them the best of luck. Hopefully we will see an English marked Dwarf in the challenges before long.

English marked Netherland Dwarf: left, the ideal; above, bred by Cliff Graveling of Norfolk. The rabbit compared to the ideal shows the difficulty with this colour. Even so, Cliff's rabbit shows some resemblance of the Dwarf characteristics and with patience and selection further improvements are possible.

CHAPTER 3
Type

PART (I)

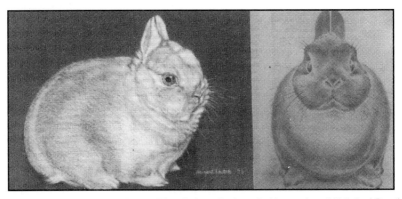

These excellent illustrations by Margaret Edwards show what is required in a good typed Netherland Dwarf

BEGINNER BREEDERS should get to know what is required to obtain good type in their stock. This is why good foundation stock with reasonably good type should be obtained from the outset.

I say reasonably good type because in my opinion it is always possible to improve type, as you start to build your stud.

It is very important at the start of your breeding programme to try and 'Fix' good type in your stock. Obviously if good type is present in the stock to start off with this will be easier. However a few bad pairings and faults will start to creep in. Initially it is better to take advice from the breeder who provided you with the stock.

Never forget that type accounts for sixty five per cent of the Netherland Dwarf rabbit. Good type is its main character. Without it we just have a small rabbit, and little else. Once good type is established in your stud, all you need is the addition of coat, colour and condition and you have a winner.

Hopefully in the following chapter we will get round to 'Fixing Type' but first a little background. Obviously the standard for the Netherland

Dwarf rabbit is man made, and where type is concerned we go against nature. Let me give you a couple of examples to explain this.

Firstly, rabbits in the wild have an elongated head and large ears which slope back. The dwarf should have a round head with ears straight up. Again the wild rabbit has strong front legs, with a streamlined body and powerful back legs built for speed. In the Dwarf we don't require speed. The body is short and compact and the front legs short and straight. As can be seen this going "Agin nature" will always pose us problems when trying to fix type. It is so easy for rabbits to be born which are throwbacks to the past. Another important point, which causes us problems when trying to breed good type, is the Polish ancestry connected to the breed. The Netherland Dwarf rabbit was created from small rabbits resembling Polish. Admittedly we have come a long way from these early creations, but they are in the breeding and a lot of poor type specimens turn up, even when breeding good type rabbits together.

We have reminders in the standard to jolt our memories about this, which I will come to later. As can be seen from the above it is not an easy task to breed good type. However, it is the main challenge for all Dwarf breeders, to fix good type and hopefully breed rabbits which will do us proud on the show table. Sometimes there is luck involved and a 'Flyer' can be bred out of the blue. However, these are few and far between. It is much better to fight nature and strive to improve type throughout the stud. By doing this, especially with the breeding does, you will increase your chances of breeding good show rabbits.

Now to the standard. I will add my own comments after each part. Please accept that these comments are strictly my opinion only. The written word in the standard is the one to follow.

We are lucky in the Dwarf standard that only a few simple words are used to state what is required. However it could be seen by some as the main reason for judges' difference of opinions. It is good that some people see things differently and it makes for a healthy Dwarf fancy. After all, if the same rabbits kept winning all the time, things could become boring, especially if the rabbit didn't belong to you.

Seriously though, a really good example of a Dwarf rabbit excelling type is accepted by almost all judges. These rabbits are a judge's delight and make all our efforts worthwhile.

Body —

Short, compact, full chested and wide shouldered devoid of raciness, front legs, short and straight.

Simple words from the Standard Book, but difficult to score all thirty points when you consider the above requirements for body is almost a third of the total points required for the dwarf. Then the importance just stands out.

My idea of a short compacted body is a rabbit that will fit in my cupped hands. If I have to stretch my fingers, even slightly, to comfortably hold the rabbit, I feel it is too long in body. I know people's hands vary in size, but if you cup your hands you get a definite round shape. If you think of roundness and circles, when visualising type in the Dwarf, you are on the right track.

Fullness and wide shouldered is a little more difficult to explain. I like to look at the Dwarf from both the front and side profiles, when judging.

When looking at the side profile, it is important to see a good roundness of chest, similar to the rump. Again think of a circle: from the front profile you need to see as much roundness as possible.

I like to see the front feet just showing, it seems to help highlight the roundness that is required. Please look at the illustrations on the first page of this chapter to see these important features.

The illustrations are from actual Dwarfs and obviously not exactly perfect. However, they do give the beginner a good idea of what is required.

Going back to perfection, I personally have never seen a perfect typed Netherland Dwarf. However over the years, particularly when judging, I have handled some excellent examples of the breed. I get a tremendous feeling of joy when handling such rabbits, but still manage to find some details not quite right. I suppose this will always be the case. The perfect specimen has yet to be born.

The part of the standard on body, that says 'devoid of raciness', is giving us a reminder of the throwback to the Polish type. Never breed from Dwarfs that have this racy characteristic. Even if put to a really good type rabbit the best you can hope for is average type rabbits.

The last little phrase on body, 'front legs short and straight', has caused a little controversy over the years. If the front legs are too long, the whole balance of the Dwarf is affected. Sometimes the legs are short enough but the rabbit tends to sit too high like a Pole. Again this is another trait which comes from the past. I personally like to see the feet just showing when the Dwarf is sitting.

I used the word balance earlier and it is a very important part of the make up of type in the Dwarf rabbit. Although the word balance is not mentioned in the standard it is very important. We will discuss this later.

Well, if your Dwarf has everything as described above it gets thirty points. You are almost a third of the way there! As can be seen from this, body type should get full attention, when selecting breeding stock. I will personally not breed off either buck or doe unless it has got good body type. Body type in does is very important. Most does of good body, will carry this feature to their progeny.

Before leaving body it is important to take into consideration the list of faults and disqualifications that affect these features.

First the faults:

Narrow Shoulders

This is a big fault in many Dwarfs. If the effort of improving this fault is not attended to, the problem just multiplies throughout the stud. If you have rabbits in your stud that have this fault, sometimes they can still be used to breed from. In the early days of forming the stud it is difficult to have everything as we want it. This is where a little common sense is required. If the fault is really bad, don't use the rabbit at all. However, if it is a doe, with just a slight narrowness of shoulder it could still be useful. Having said that this rabbit needs to be bred to a stud buck excelling body. If you have not got one seek a mating to the best you can find.

This cross matching method is a good way to progress in your early days of establishing a stud. The really important part of this operation comes when assessing the results of the mating. This is where serious selection is needed.

I would not advise keeping any offspring for future breeding that has not improved in body. I would still consider taking the same doe to another buck, but if this failed to show an improvement, its future as a breeder would be over. The above is a sound way to attempt to improve any faults, but you have to be ruthless in your selection of future breeding stock.

I know I keep saying go for a mating to a good buck, but this is a sure way of progressing. However, please concentrate on preferably one breeder only, as by going to different strains of Dwarfs, other problems could start to creep in. Too many strains mixed together can just throw up more faults. It is better to learn from one breeder at the beginning.

Always look for the opportunity to buy stock off this breeder, especially if improvements are being made through the matings you have had.

Disqualification, racy type and crooked legs.

Rabbits with the above faults should never be used for breeding, full stop. Racy type is again a trait from the past and please make sure that's where it remains. Crooked legs is a little more difficult to explain. It can be a result of breeding off unhealthy stock, or through close inbreeding. If it appears where inbreeding and linebreeding has been taking place it is a very good reminder that you need an outcross quick. Unfortunately it always seems to be a very good rabbit that throws up this fault, but it has no use whatsoever in the breeding programme.

Please don't be put off inbreeding and linebreeding by the above. Once you have started to establish your stud, it is a very useful tool to fix the desired qualities in detail.

Head.

Round and broad skull scores fifteen points.

Well what could be simpler than that? Easy to say; but head faults are one of the most common problems in the Dwarf. Please note that it does not say big head.

The head should appear round from all angles, especially round the muzzle and top skull areas.

In some strains, heads are very slow to develop and some Dwarfs are occasionally up to eighteen months old before head development has finished. Whilst again in other strains where there is a little more wealth of coat, heads develop earlier.

I once plunged three of my stud bucks in water on a very hot day. When wet their heads were the same shape and size. However, one of these rabbits excelled head to the other two when they were dry.

Again, when rabbits start to moult the heads don't look as good until they appear full coated again. I also like to see good width of skull between the eyes. I look for this width between the eyes when sorting

Above: this Marten Sable exhibited by Nigel Atkinson shows a good balance of type features. Note the bold eye and good pose. A smart exhibit from one of the top studs

out a litter of youngsters. The ones with good width between the eyes at this stage, usually end up with good heads.

Head size to me is not very important providing that it balances with the body. There we are, the word balance again!

The listed fault just says narrow face. This is the exact opposite of what I said previously. Rabbits that have this fault are of no use in the breeding pen. It is a fault that relates to the past and spoils the overall character of the breed.

Ears

Erect, of good substance, well furred, slightly rounded at tips. Desired length 50mm or 2 inches.

This scores fifteen points.

I must say at this point, that when I am judging very few rabbits score all fifteen points. A big majority of present day Dwarfs have one of the listed faults: some have all three. It is very difficult to 'fix' good ears in your stock but well worth the effort.

First the word erect. Dwarf ears should be upright and straight on the head. Sometimes the ears are sloping back. This is usually when the Dwarf is sitting too high or throwing its head back. (More about this later.) Also, the ears should be straight all the way up, with no bends or kinks etc.

A lot is said about ear setting in judges reports. The Dwarfs' ears should be set on top of the head, roughly in line with the back of the eye circle, or to say almost in line with it. In this position they give a good balance to the head. That is, of course, providing they fulfil the other requirements.

The terms: of 'good substance' and 'slightly rounded at tips', for our purposes can be discussed together. Both requirements seem to run hand in hand.

Invariably, the rabbit with the pointed ears usually has poor ear substance. These combined faults are very difficult to eradicate in the breeding pen.

The simplest solution to start off with is don't mate together two rabbits with the same ear fault. Better still, mate a rabbit that is defective in one ear fault to one that excels in this feature. This cross matching is a slow process, but be patient, it works. You should, however, keep an eye on the same fault in the next generation.

Slow improvement is sometimes better. It gives you time to control the undesired element.

"Well furred". Sometimes this can be a difficult one. As the rabbit matures, ear coverage should slowly improve. However, if it doesn't it could be something hereditary in the strain.

Try to improve this, because it spoils the overall appearance of the rabbit, especially from a judge's point of view.

Desired Ear Length 50mm (2")

This is easier to control and again adds to the overall appearance of the Dwarf. When judging I use the second joint of my forefinger as a guide to ear length.

By doing this I am being fair to the exhibit, as this length is just a fraction above two inches.

Sometimes breeding does that have overlength ears can still be useful. However, they should have good carriage and substance. Always mate these does to bucks with correct ear length and as good on ear quality as possible.

Now back to these listed faults. Although the effects of these have just been discussed, they are worth mentioning again. The reason for this is that the majority of judges penalise Netherland Dwarfs with these faults very heavily. And rightly so.

The faults are: **ears not erect, bent or overlength**. A good idea is to write these faults down, where they can be seen, in your shed. By doing this when you are selecting stock for breeding, you have a constant reminder of what is NOT required.

Eyes

Round, bold, bright, of good colour, five points. A simple requirement but again another feature that gives the breed its character. There is nothing better than to see a round, bold eye, full of brightness. It seems to set the head off better and adds to the overall appearance of the Dwarf rabbit.

Some strains have bolder eyes than others, but even so in most strains rabbits with bold eyes turn up sooner or later.

Certain colours of Dwarf have a bolder eye than others. Agouties are particularly noted for this. In classes where competition is fairly even, boldness of eye can be the decider. So although only five points are allocated to this feature, its importance should always be high on the list of requirements for good type.

Well, that's the target. Unfortunately we have to get all these requirements on one rabbit.

This is the most difficult thing to do where type is concerned.

It is no good having a good body if the rabbit fails head and ears. What we have got to do is achieve the right balance of all the type features. This is always difficult to explain in words, but here goes.

Head to body balance is a term I use in judges reports. What I look for is both head and body to be in proportion to each other.

I have heard it explained as a tangerine on a small Orange. Or a small circle on a larger circle. This is in fact what we are after with no neck visible at all.

Again it is no good having a big head if the body is big and long.

Once we have got head to body balance firmly fixed in our minds, and in our Dwarfs as well, all we need is ears and eyes in the right place and proportion and we are there.

Never forget that head, ears and eyes score thirty five points, which is a third of what is required. So if ears are correctly placed on a good shaped head, together with bold eye, we are well on the way. Add to this an excellent shaped body, proportionately balanced to the above and we are there!

At this point it is appropriate to mention the way the Dwarf is required to sit, when being judged.

Again it is not mentioned in the standard, but when posed correctly the Dwarf can show the correct balance of type required.

The Dwarf needs to be trained to sit up slightly to show the roundness of chest required. Ears should be held straight at the same time. Again it is nice to see a little front feet.

Rabbits that sit too high, like a Pole, spoil their balance. Front legs look long and sometimes heads and ears slope back.

It would be good if we had a full scale model showing exactly the balance - type - proportions required in the ideal Dwarf.

A lovely three quarter pose showing good balance of type features

CHAPTER 4
More on Type

PART (II)

IN THE LAST CHAPTER I mentioned cross matching as a method of eliminating or improving faults.

To recap, this is where you use a rabbit that excels in a certain feature, say head, to a rabbit that fails in the same.

Obviously the idea is to select rabbits in the resulting litter that show an improvement on the fault.

Unfortunately, it is not just that easy. We need to do more than concentrate on one feature at a time if we are to improve type as a whole.

This is where life gets difficult for the breeder, because we need to take the **cross matching** method a stage further in order to progress.

What we need to do is to get as many good features as possible on one rabbit. This gives us a better chance to transfer these good qualities to the next generation.

By far the best rabbit to use in this situation is the **stud buck**. Over the years I have placed great importance on this rabbit. If he is a good one, he will become the king pin of your stud. However, if he is not good enough he can so easily ruin all your efforts.

I have said earlier in the book that your stud buck will probably breed more rabbits in a season than any of your does. Therefore the chances of 'like breeding like' multiplies the more he is used.

What I look for in a stud buck is good balance between head and body, with good ears and eye.

He has got to be well within the weight limit, ideally around 2lb 2 oz. (Alright, I can hear you saying, this is what we all want. But these are the ideals we should strive for.)

If you look at this rabbit critically, you will still find something wrong with him. Perhaps he could be a little bolder in the head, or maybe his ears could be carried better. Even the top class stud buck will have a little something wrong with him.

However, these faults should only be slight ones. The least faults you have on your balanced or primary stud buck, the easier it will be to make further progress.

If your buck has the slight faults we covered previously, what you need is one or maybe two more bucks to complete the picture.

Aim for one that excels head and one that excels ears. (If you can get one that excels both these features, better still.) Either it or they will become your secondary stud bucks. It is very important that these bucks do not have any outstanding body faults.

If these secondary bucks are of the same strain or breeding, the chance of further improvement becomes easier.

The next step is to use to the full your breeding does' potential.

Does that are bred out of the balanced, or primary stud buck and that have very similar faults to him, need to be taken to the buck that excels in the departments they lack.

Say the fault is ears. If the does bred from the mating show a marked improvement, they can be taken back to the balanced or primary stud buck.

What you are doing by the above is utilising the **cross matching** method, to get more good type features on one rabbit, as each generation progresses.

Always be on the lookout for a young buck that is better than your primary stud buck. He will eventually replace him if he is good enough, especially if he has been bred by the primary stud buck.

At this point it would be appropriate to discuss the weight of the Dwarf and how this can affect your progress. Bucks that are well up to the weight limit can pose us a problem if used as stud bucks.

This is especially so if the rabbit has to be dieted to keep within the weight limit. Such rabbits usually fail condition and if fed properly would be well over the weight limit.

These bucks should not be used for breeding, as these weight problems will recur in future generations.

Condition is really important in trying to improve type. Firm, solid flesh overall makes the rabbit feel better and looks rounder when handled.

Rabbits that are just below the weight limit, with extremely good condition, could still be useful as stud bucks. If the rabbit has good balance of type, he may pass this on to his offspring.

However, I would only consider using such a buck on a temporary basis. As soon as he has bred a rabbit with the same quality for balance, but smaller, he should be replaced.

Early Creations

As I have written in an earlier chapter, we have come a long way since the early creations, that first occurred as Dwarf rabbits.

Those early Dwarfs(?) were the result of a mutation gene for Dwarfism (Dw). This specific gene seems to have an effect on the pituitary gland. One of the secretions of this gland is growth hormone. The activity of this mutation gene has reduced the growth hormone.

From this, a rabbit has evolved with the typical Netherland Dwarf features. The main characters of this are: small round head, bold eye, small erect ears and compact body.

This heterozygote gene gives us the shape and size of the Netherland Dwarf we see today.

Unfortunately certain undesirable qualities are found in the homozygous form. This is a double dose of the gene (Dw Dw) and is **lethal**.

Study of Birth Sizes

Well, enough of the technical jargon. Let us look in simple terms at how this can help us in the breeding pen.

The simplest way of explaining the workings of these genes is by making a study of birth sizes of the Dwarf rabbit.

The first size baby we come across is very small and looks premature. It usually has a very large head, compared to body, with a pronounced forehead. These babies are usually only about two inches long, or less. They have a double dose of the gene (Dw Dw) and are lethal babies. They usually don't survive more than a few days, and are perhaps better destroyed at birth.

Next to look at is the normal type birth, size about three inches long. This is the heterozygous type with a gene combination (Dw dw). This gives us the show type dwarf we all try to breed.

From these show type specimens we get our show rabbits, stud bucks and future breeding does.

Obviously it is in all our interests to breed this type in large numbers in order to improve our studs.

Next we have the youngster that is a lot larger than the normal birth size. This has the gene combination (dw dw) and for our purposes we will call it pet/breeder type.

This type of rabbit grows very big and does not show the typical dwarf characteristics required. However, sometimes a doe from this type can be useful for our requirements.

Hence pet/breeder type, or some call it **breeder selected** small rabbit. Now let's get down to making the above types work to our advantage.

The first type, the lethal babies, are of no use to us whatsoever. They are purely an unfortunate bi product of the mutation gene set up. Some breeders call these babies peanuts because of their size. I have also heard them called jelly babies.

Personally I don't mind seeing these babies appear in my stock. They show me that the Dwarf Gene is present. But their numbers need to be kept under control - more about this shortly.

Before leaving this type of gene combination, it is important to say that they can only appear if **both parents** carry the (Dw) gene.

The next type, the normal birth size (Dw dw) is the one we want to perpetuate most of all. If these show type rabbits are bred together and each of their parents carry one of the (Dw) genes, the average results are usually as follows:

In a litter of four you can usually expect one lethal, one pet/breeder and two show types.

This is not a bad average but you can improve this further still.

Before we come to that, let us look at the pet/breeder type (dw dw). If rabbits of this type are bred together, no show type rabbits will be produced. We just breed more rabbits of similar type with less and less of the true characteristic of the Netherland Dwarf.

However, now we come to the most important part of utilising the dwarf gene for our purposes. This involves using a pet/breed type (dw dw) but it MUST be a doe.

Obviously the doe will be a big one and I use the affectionate term of "ugly doe" for this rabbit.

It is important to have as good a body shape as possible on this doe. This rabbit is best bred to your best or primary stud buck.

This rabbit will obviously be show type and ideally should be prepotent.

The results in a litter of four, are usually as follows: two show type and two pet/breeder, with no lethal babies.

Sometimes because of her size the doe, especially if very fertile, will produce more youngsters. This is a bonus.

If your stud buck is a 'carrier' of the lethal gene (Dw Dw), sometimes a bigger percentage of show type rabbits will appear.

The beauty of using the pet/breeder type doe is that less fatalities occur, because of the absence of the lethal babies.

In a stud of say ten does, it is useful to have say two 'ugly does' as part of the breeding team.

Sometimes it is a fruitful exercise to cross over the show types bred from both ugly does. The buck of this selected pair from the ugly does, is maybe one you are using for the first time. Try this, the results may surprise you.

I have used these 'ugly does' in my breeding plans for many years, long before I fully understood the technical workings of the gene. When using this method of breeding, it is important to get the balance right, and avoid breeding too many lethal babies. If done patiently and carefully many show type Dwarfs will be bred, with good type qualities. Again the key word is selection of breeding stock.

When talking about the stud buck earlier I mentioned "prepotent".

This prepotency is another attribute that can be used carefully to improve type in the Dwarf rabbit. A rabbit with this quality has the capacity to produce specimens better than itself and in greater numbers.

If your stud buck has this quality and is near the standard, you are lucky to own an animal that could be worth his weight in gold in the breeding pen.

I have heard many breeders over the years who have said that they own a doe which breeds good stock, whichever buck it is bred to. Obviously these does will be extremely useful as breeders, but more important still, they could be rabbits that could breed a buck with the **prepotent** quality.

Many years ago I did an experiment with two brothers bred from a doe which had this quality. One particular season these bucks were mated to the same numbers of selected does in turn. The end product being that one of the bucks bred far more quality rabbits than the other.

This proved that he was more prepotent than his brother. (Just for the record, this buck was not as good a rabbit as his brother, which shows that this prepotent quality can be hidden.)

Obviously it is not easy to breed these exceptional animals, and furthermore I am not saying that everybody should try the same experiment.

However, always be on the lookout for such an animal coming through the stud. He can become the cornerstone of your stud. If his potential is found early enough, he could be responsible for many generations of excellent Dwarf rabbits.

The best I have bred was a Siamese Sable I called Exodus. He quickly established a very good stud of Siamese and Marten Sables for me. Stock which was sold on also did well and rabbits from this strain won many best in shows at the highest level. This proved that prepotency can be carried to future generations.

In recent years I have been lucky enough to breed two black bucks that had this quality. Unfortunately, one died before his full potential was realised.

I am sure one or two present day R.E.W. breeders have these prepotent bucks, because the quality of these animals is exceptional at present.

Unfortunately, it is the rarer colours that need bucks with this prepotent quality. Well, somewhere along the line, using the breeding patterns mentioned above, related stock will have been bred together.

This beautiful dark Marten Sable shows required type characteristic to the full

This of course is inbreeding and as I have said before, it can be utilised to our advantage in the breeding pen. It is definitely one of the most important ways to improve and fix good type in our stock.

Before discussing this subject more fully, it is important to look at all aspects of the Dwarf rabbit.

CHAPTER 5
Condition

CONDITION in the Netherland Dwarf rabbit is probably more important than in any other breed. Its diminutive size means that good condition should be paramount in order to live up to the requirements of the breeder and exhibitor. These requirements are firstly *General condition*, which contributes to the general well being of our rabbits; secondly *Breeding condition*, which we need in order to perpetuate and improve our stock. Then we have *Show condition*, which gives us that little bit extra and provides us with outstanding winners.

Before discussing these three requirements further it is important to say that if good common sense, observation and well balanced diet are put in operation, *good condition* follows. The standard only allocates ten points for condition. However when you consider that good type, colour and coat all depend on *good condition*, the points just add that little bit extra. The standard just states the following: *Condition, firm in flesh, good coat, and free from any disease.*

The above few words are really what it is all about.

Firm in Flesh. The flesh over the back end of the rabbit should feel hard. No hip bone should be felt. Also, flesh should be firm around the rib cage and chest area. Feeling bones when a Dwarf is handled is usually an indication that attention to feeding and diet is required. More about feeding and nutrition later.

Rabbits in this hardy condition are able to cope better with the stresses we place on them. Examples of this are obviously Breeding, Showing, Moulting or times when a rabbit is subject to change in Environment.

Good Coat. Rabbits that are in a healthy condition have a shine and lustre to their coat. If the coat is moult-free but is dull and stares at you, it is an indication that something is wrong. Before rushing off to the vet, observe this closely. Is the rabbit eating and drinking? Is it moving around freely?

Observation of your stock is really important. When you have finished feeding your rabbits, stand for ten minutes looking, listening and generally observing your stock. Something spotted during this observation can sometimes be remedied before a problem occurs.

A good example that springs to mind is the *blocked drinker*. The rabbit cannot get water, so it won't eat and the day after looks off colour. If left it would deteriorate rapidly. So unblock the drinker: soon no problem. This is one example of observation. Probably if you can't stand ten minutes looking over your stock, you have got too many rabbits.

Free from any disease. This is a very difficult one for judges, because after all we are not Veterinary Surgeons. Sometimes a rabbit could be carrying a disease which shows no visible signs. The way of interpreting this is as follows. Simply, I examine everything on the rabbit where there is a hole. Eyes, nose, ears, vent area. If all is OK and the rabbit looks generally healthy it passes.

Before leaving the standard it is important to discuss the disqualifications which relate to *condition*.

There are three. Not in a condition of health to be judged, running eyes and overgrown or mutilated teeth.

The first one is easy. If a rabbit fails the test outlined above when discussing *free from any disease*, it is sent back to its pen. If I considered the *condition* could affect other rabbits at the show, I would insist it be boxed and taken outside the show hall. Obviously this is a situation none of us wants, so always thoroughly inspect your stock before showing.

The simple checks will avoid judges having to make any unpleasant decisions.

Always try to show your stock in perfect health. Never forget that the stress suffered by a rabbit that is shown in poor condition could actually kill it.

Overgrown or mutilated teeth is a problem that has been with us for a long time and will continue to be one. It is the result of the Dwarf characteristic of the head shape.

Nearly all Dwarf breeders have come across this condition. In fact sometimes the better the quality of the Dwarf the more likelihood there is of getting this problem. Never forget overgrown teeth is hereditary. If you breed off a Dwarf with this disqualification fault you will make the problem worse. Simply, do not breed off it, or sell a rabbit with bad teeth! All right, a rabbit's teeth can be cut, but it is something that usually needs to be done regularly for the rest of its life.

The rabbit is better humanely destroyed.

I know this is a touchy subject, but there are times when this course of action is required. I personally think this is part and parcel of stock management, but that is strictly my opinion.

Veterinary Surgeons are very costly where this is concerned. I assure you, however, that if you can't bring yourself to learn how to humanely kill a rabbit, there are fanciers around who can help you.

If the rabbit is a pet and has overgrown teeth and you want to keep it, learn how to cut its teeth and everything is OK.

From an exhibition point of view however, they are of no use whatsoever. Sometimes rabbits that have perfectly good teeth can be 'carriers' of this fault. If you are getting a lot of teeth problems this could be the cause.

Finding the culprit that is the carrier can sometimes be difficult, but it is well worth the effort. There is nothing worse than to keep breeding Dwarfs of good quality with this recurring problem.

Next, **running eyes**, another problem that occurs at some time or another with the majority of Dwarf breeders. If a Dwarf's eye is running when judged it should be disqualified. If the problem is simple it can sometimes be cleared up quite easily. Just by placing the rabbit in a different hutch can prove to be successful.

What you have got to watch for is persistent running eyes, because sometimes these can never be cured.

When the rabbit's eye first starts to run, it may be better trying a few simple remedies before rushing off to the Vet. If the changing-hutch routine doesn't work, look for signs of infection. If the eye is still running but there is no sign of infection, try bathing with cold tea, or use a tea bag soaked in cold water as a compress.

If this old wives' remedy fails, sometimes eye drops that have been used to treat conjunctivitis can be used successfully.

It is possible that too much protein in the diet can be the cause of running eyes.

If simple remedies fail, a trip to the vet may be needed. If after veterinary treatment the eye keeps running, again we may be looking at a possibility of persistent running eye. Rabbits that have this condition can pass it on to their offspring.

I would not use a Dwarf for breeding that has this problem.

Sometimes this persistent eye problem is confused with *overgrown back teeth*. In this situation the *teeth problem* is usually causing the tear ducts to block, and the result is continually running eyes.

Rabbits like this should not be used for breeding.

Well, that's the nasty side over with. Let's get down to ways we can ensure our charges can keep in the best possible health, so that hopefully they have a good enough immune system to fight off disease.

I am of the firm opinion that keeping stock in a good sound healthy condition is a combination of a well balanced diet, stock management and observation.

Before discussing feeding it is really important that our Dwarfs receive a clean fresh supply of water at all times. With modern day feeds as they are, in all different types and forms, a consistent supply of water is a must.

It helps the rabbit to eat properly and ensures it gets the best nutritional value out of the food. Actually, present day breeding, with the different mixes on the market, make good nutritional feeding easier than ever.

At this point, I would like to go through how I feed my own stock, and hopefully some of it can be of help to the beginner.

I am a great believer in variety as regards feeding livestock. Rabbits in the wild eat virtually anything and in fact sometimes they have to. It is a good idea to try to imitate the ways of the wild rabbit.

My basic food consists of 2.5 parts good quality rabbit mix to one part rabbit pellets. This I mix in a small bucket to which I add two handfuls of pigeon conditioner. This is the mixture I feed to the stock all the year round.

By good rabbit mix, I mean one that contains as many different items of cereal and corn as possible. Preferably I like to see both the rabbit mix and the pellets dust free.

My adult Dwarfs get just less than 2oz of this mix a day. Rabbits over the age of eight weeks are housed on their own and fed as adults.

During stressful times of the year, like moulting time, I add the following to the full bucket of food: a handful each of peanuts, flake maize and sunflower seeds. Because this mix contains very oily ingredients, I sometimes give a little less quantity of food at feeding time.

When the rabbits have moulted out and the winter months get closer, I go back to the original mix. Rabbits seem to delight in crushing hard corn and it keeps them fit.

I also feed good quality organic-grown first crop hay to my Dwarfs. This is fed to the stock all the year round, but only in small quantities. I have found that once rabbits lie on the hay they don't eat it as readily. This is where I imitate nature with my stock.

Hay that is naturally grown is very similar to food that is eaten in the wild. I avoid hay that has been grown by fertilisers. Those types of hay are grown very quickly and have to be dried correctly before storage. They can sometimes result in tummy troubles if fed too early, especially to young stock.

Most of my rabbits will eat hay before they go to their mix, they seem to know it's good for them. I treat them all as individuals: rabbits that are good hay eaters get a little extra and so on.

This again is the observation part of stock management and the rabbits benefit from it. My stock is fed six days a week: on the seventh no food is given.

Obviously does with youngsters are fed and watered, but nothing else. On this day I add Vanodine V18 to the drinking water. It is an Iodine complex disinfectant and is perfectly safe in the drinking water, provided you follow the right dosage. It seems to help clear the stock out and does them good.

Whilst back on the subject of water, I have noticed my rabbits drink very little. However, they are consistent with their consumption of water. I don't feed any greens, so the only fluctuation is in very hot weather, and when does are feeding.

Over the years I have come to associate this consistency of water intake as a barometer to health. If any of the stock suddenly changes its drinking habits either more or less, it is usually an indication that something is wrong. Also water is an good remedy for administering medicines and additives.

The only additives I use in the diet are occasionally vitamin and mineral supplements. When any of my stock go off colour, I add these to the water. They are also good at times of heavy stress.

An example of this is when a rabbit is showing the strain after a long day at a show. I use children's tonic foods in these situations. The best being Minadex, but Metatone is also very good. They act as a sort of pick-me-up and usually get the rabbit back to normal eating patterns. Minadex has an orange flavour to it, I just colour the bottle drinker and rabbits are happy to take it.

Feeding times are another situation where I try to copy nature. I have noticed over the years that rabbits seem to do most of their eating from evening time onwards.

This is the time I feed my rabbits. The exception are does with litters or youngsters running together who also get a feed at morning. Rabbits seem to like set times for eating. An old fancier friend, no longer with us, used to feed his stock when it started going dark.

Obviously the times changed as the seasons progressed, but his stock was always very lively when he entered the shed to feed. This liveliness on entering the shed to feed is a good time for a quick observation of your stock. Two minutes just looking round your stock is sometimes enough to find a rabbit not quite up to the mark.

Feed this rabbit first and observe it all the time you are doing the rest of your feeding. I can enter my shed many times a day, but the rabbits seem to know instinctively when it is feeding time. Probably this is because I talk to them whilst feeding.

Strict feeding routines can play an important part in the well being of your stock. I have a tendency to treat my stock as individuals.

Some rabbits will eat their favourite item of food from my hand. A lot of them seem to have different food items as their favourite. This is where a varied content of the mix is very important. It gives the rabbit more opportunity to find its favourite food.

I am not a nutrition expert. There are many brands of rabbit food on the market, also many experts to make sure the nutrition is right.

If you have a good balance of fibre, fat, carbohydrate and protein in the mix, rabbits have everything they need with the addition of water, to have a really healthy life.

Another important aspect of feeding is consistency. If you are feeding on similar lines to the above and all is well, don't change! Rabbits hate sudden change in their diets and can just stop eating, with obvious consequences. If you have to change anything, like feeding for different times of the year, do it gradually. If you are introducing a particular ingredient for the fist time, start by putting a good handful in a bucket of mix. Then next time put two in and so on.

This slow introduction gives the rabbits time to get used to the new ingredient. If you buy in new stock, get some food off the seller. You will have enough problems getting the rabbit used to the new environment, without having a rabbit that will not eat. It is easy to get a rabbit to your way of feeding, just do it gradually.

Feeding on similar lines to the above, Dwarfs should be fit but not put weight on, or be fat. Size in the Netherland Dwarf rabbit is down to good breeding and should have nothing to do with feeding.

This leads me to another important aspect of management which in turn plays a big part in the condition of your stock. This is the amount of hutch space a rabbit needs to grow and exercise, in order to achieve the condition of fitness required. At this point, as with feeding, I can only relate to you the methods I use.

I use two sizes of hutches. 24" x 24" for does and 18" x 24" for bucks. From eight weeks of age, stock that has been retained for either breeding or showing are housed individually. Placing a doe in a 24" x 24" cage at eight weeks old looks a little bit daunting. However after a few days she is soon skipping around the hutch, eating well and getting plenty of exercise. This is the hutch she stays in either till she has finished breeding or is sold.

Young bucks are placed in the 18" x 24" hutches. These are also used sometimes for weaning a litter, which is kept together from six to eight weeks old. I find the Dwarfs' growth rate is very steady in these conditions.

The combination of good breeding and plenty of exercise gets the rabbits in really hard condition. This is especially so in the winter months when no heating is used whatsoever.

By the time the does are five months old or thereabouts they come into breeding condition. The bucks are usually a little later, perhaps about six months old. This is the part of Dwarf breeding I really enjoy. We are on the next verge of the next generation of Dwarfs, and the excitement of planning matings etc, can't be explained in words.

When this stage is reached the doe has her first full coat and usually can't keep still. Tell tale signs are constantly digging in the bedding, and she may even start 'carrying' and play at nest making. On inspection her vulva will be a dark red going to a purple colour. It is also sometimes swollen, indicating her readiness to breed. Irrespective of age, it is my advice to get her mated as soon as possible. She will probably be at the most fertile period of her life.

Signs of the bucks approaching breeding condition are usually similar to the does. He is usually full coated by this time, and at the peak of condition. Like the doe he won't be able to keep still. His movements are usually side to side of the hutch. On feeding he may brush your hand out of the way, or rub his chin on you, or everything also for that matter. On close inspection his testicles should be well down and he is ready for breeding. Usually the only thing to quieten him down is mating him to a doe.

Breeding, rearing and fertility is covered later in the book.

For now, however, it is enough to say that rabbits in this condition should be at the peak of fitness. They need to be able to cope with all the hard work that is in store for them, especially the does. The ultimate condition to strive for without doubt, is show condition.

To get a closer look at what is required let's look at the rabbit through the judge's eyes. He will look for a rabbit that is disease free, with good solid body condition. As he handles the rabbit, besides assessing its coat, type and colour qualities he will be looking for brightness of eye and general alertness of the animal.

If the rabbit handles well, doesn't jump about all over the place, he will be impressed and look at it more closely. Most of the time the judges at this stage are trying to find something wrong. This will be difficult if the rabbit is of good quality and in excellent show condition. Its coat will be moult free and shining. Claws will be trim and if the rabbit is white or has white underparts, it will be spotlessly clean.

Usually the longer the judge looks at an exhibit, the more he is impressed. Next thing you know the rabbit is placed at the top of the table and stays there. Rabbits of this quality don't just win best of breed but go on to Best in Show.

How can we as exhibitors get these requirements?

The first part is easy. We have checked at home that the rabbit is disease-free and fit to show. The good solid body condition and brightness of eye and alert expression is down to our excellent feeding and management routine.

The rabbit has obviously got good type, coat and colour or we would

A Netherland Dwarf in superb condition, showing lustre of coat and shining bright eyes. A judge's delight!

not be showing it. Of course our rabbit has been handled at home on a very regular basis. It is used to settling quietly, showing itself off and posing. Obviously we have got the rabbit used to being handled by judges. We have even gone to the extreme of studying how different judges handle rabbits.

We know the rabbit finished moulting about two weeks ago. Since then, he has been groomed for a short time daily. All the dead hair has been removed form his coat, even his belly. When he finished moulting we trimmed his claws, so everything should be fine. We know he is really clean because we have worked hard at this. When his show potential was realised a few months ago we made a special effort to make sure his hutch was kept clean at all times. On the occasion that he dirtied himself, we took the advice of other fanciers. One fancier told us to wash the rabbit's feet and dry off with cornflour.

We then placed him in a travelling box for a while, obviously with clean white shavings in it. Besides keeping him clean this method really got him used to the travelling box. In fact we have occasionally taken him for a ride in the car and on arriving home we handled him a lot. This will get him used to show-biz.

Another fancier told us to use a chalk block on his feet regularly; this seems to work OK. The most bizarre thing we have been told, is to wet the soiled feet of the rabbit with saliva. This we tried and applied it with a toothbrush. The rabbit tried to remove the human smell from himself by licking and cleaning the soiled part at the same time. This fancier told us to watch a class of rabbits after they have been judged and replaced in their pens.

Sure enough they all started to lick and groom themselves, trying to remove the human smell from themselves. The saliva trick is good if a rabbit dirties himself on the day of the show. In fact, the rabbit did this today, but when we got to the show, he had cleaned himself up.

Well, we have left nothing to chance, and have even cleaned and brushed the inside of our rabbit's front feet. We have found a small suede brush to be very good for this necessary little operation.

Well, back to the judging, fingers crossed he has nearly finished handling our rabbit. The judge seems to have been looking at him for ages. There he is placed at the top of the table. There is nothing else to touch him. Best of Breed, Best Fancy and then Best in Show. What a feeling, all the hard work has been really worthwhile.

Bradford Championship Show, here we come!

Well, fairy tale over, let's get back to reality. It is possible for a tip top Dwarf (see photo on facing page) to go Best in Show at Bradford (the Fancy's top annual Championship Show) in fact it was achieved for the second time in January 1997 when Mr & Mrs George Evans took Best in Show with their Red Eyed White "Moston Man".

This chapter has described show condition and with a little effort and the help of nature, the fairy tale can become reality.

One of the most photographed Netherland Dwarfs in recent years: taken from the
cover of *Fur & Feather* this is Moston One Man, a Red Eyed White buck owned by
Mr & Mrs George Evans, sitting in the famous Rose Bowl awarded to best in show
at Bradford Championship Show 1997. This rabbit is probably the best
Netherland Dwarf I have judged in the last five years.

CHAPTER 6

Coat

COAT in the Netherland Dwarf is a very important feature and its special requirements make it a vital characteristic of the breed. To me, if everything on the Dwarf is good, the right coat adds the finishing touch. Dwarfs with a moult-free, excellent roll back coat will challenge for top honours at any show.

First let us look at what is required by the standard and then expand on this a little. As with all features of the standard only a few words explain what is required: i.e.

Coat, Soft, Short, Dense, Roll Back

Very simple words but difficult to explain, easily, the exact requirements.

First, SOFT. Obviously the only way you can judge this feature is by touch. I know sense of touch can vary from person to person but the Dwarf coat should always have a soft, silky texture. This should be apparent whichever way the coat is stroked.

Next, SHORT. Unfortunately the standard does not say how long the coat should be. I have found over the years that ½ inch in length is long enough to give us the requirements where coat is concerned.

Now, DENSE. The amount of underfur present in the coat is what gives us the required density.

Finally, ROLLBACK. The most difficult part of the coat requirement to explain and also just as difficult to get it on the rabbit.

This feature is one of the true characteristics of the Dwarf rabbit. It is a must to fix it in your stock (simply, rollback means that the coat should go back, slowly, to its original position when stroked rump to neck).

Actually the combination of the first three words SOFT, SHORT and DENSE all contribute to the required rollback feature. What the standard does not mention are guard hairs.

This type of hair, which is sharper tipped and longer than the underfur, is present in all breeds of rabbit except Rex.

Where the Dwarf is concerned the balance of length, guard hairs and undercoat is what gives us the required roll-back coat.

Let me give three examples of what can occur in the Dwarf coat.

The first is the "dead" or open coat. In this situation coat length is usually O.K. and plenty of dense underfur is present. Unfortunately, there are not enough guard hairs to give us the required texture to rollback.

Please do not be confused with moult. When a Dwarf is naturally moulting the above type of coat can occur sometimes during the moulting operation. However, when the rabbit has achieved full coat it should have acquired the rollback feature again.

More about moulting later.

The second example is what we call the flyback coat. This is almost a reverse of the open coat.

This coat is usually a touch longer with an abundance of guard hairs and hardly any underfur. When stroked the coat literally flies away from the hand. Fly back coat is listed in the standard as a fault. Unfortunately, it is a trait from the past and resembles the Polish style coat.

The final example is the correct rollback coat. In this situation the balance of underfur to guard hair is proportionally correct and the result is the rollback coat. It is a coat unlike most fancy rabbits and is a beautiful characteristic of the breed.

Before leaving the standard, good coat is also a requirement for condition. This makes coat as important as condition in order to fulfil both requirements.

That is the standard for coat, now let us look at some finer points. The reason I stressed, earlier, the importance of coat is because it can affect other features of the standard.

First Point: TYPE. In recent years, especially in R.E.W.'s, a slightly heavier, longer and denser coat has evolved in some strains.

Although the slightly longer coat detracts from the rollback coat, the overall type appearance can look better.

The extra wealth of coat, especially round the head and jowels make the Dwarf look more attractive in type features. This type of Dwarf sometimes can put judges into a bit of a dilemma. The few points a Dwarf loses on coat means little to the number of points it can appear to gain on type. Obviously, it is times like these when judges see things differently.

Sometimes the extra wealth of coat makes the Dwarf look a little bulky even though it is well within the weight limit. This is where the word 'balance' becomes very important.

Most judges look for the best balanced Dwarf, including all aspects of the standard. The little variations in the different strains of Dwarf just makes judging more interesting. Interpretation of the different judges, where the slight variations occur, makes for a healthy Dwarf Fancy.

As well as type, coat can affect colour quality. In the coat of the Dwarf it is the guard hair that is chiefly responsible for good colour.

If the rabbit has a slightly sharper guard hair the chances are that colour will be better than on other exhibits.

The fly back type of coat usually has excellent colour. Obviously we do not want this, because at the expense of good colour we have a big fault on coat. However with very careful selection it is possible to get the sharper guard hair present in the correct rollback coat.

This combination of good coat and colour can usually be the decider in a very even class of Dwarfs. Really it is all about balance again.

It is pointless improving coat at the expense of colour and vice-versa. The age of the coat can also affect colour. If the rabbit is almost due to moult, especially if it is a second year rabbit, colour will be past its best. The reason for this is because the coat has received wear and tear for almost twelve months.

When you see judges reports saying "over the top", "needs to moult", or "dull colour" this is what they are usually referring to. Once the rabbit has had a good clean moult, colour will again be back at its best.

If I can just give a little tip at this point, when a rabbit has finished its moult, just give it two or three weeks for the 'bloom' to come before you start showing again.

Well, we have nicely got round to the subject of moult. Before we discuss this further however, I would like to look at how the development of the growing youngsters affects coat.

From day one until the rabbit is about five months of age the Dwarf's coat is continually changing. Sometimes this continual changing of coat can affect the appearance of the Dwarf. Occasionally the 'ugly duckling' can make a swan. Unfortunately the reverse can take place.

In the first few days of life coat is very important. The quicker coat starts to grow, especially around winter time, the more the chance of survival. Also if the doe was in good coat there is more chance of a mound of bubbling fur.

Never be afraid of pulling more fur from the doe in order to protect the valuable youngsters, whilst at their most vulnerable stage of life. I will do virtually anything to ensure a live litter survives. More about this in a later chapter.

Well, back to coat development. At the three or four day stage all the youngsters should be covered in a good layer of guard hairs. At the eye opening stage there is more coat still. I usually think that this is the stage where they are no longer prone to chilling. However there is a long way to go.

Around the three to four weeks stage the youngsters have started to explore the outside world. The baby coat is about half grown, ears are pricked up and they all look like winners.

About the six week stage they have plenty of baby coat and are at a good age for quality assessment. From this stage onwards new coat can start to grow.

At around twelve weeks old youngsters usually have enough new coat to be assessed by a judge. Judges do not usually penalise young Dwarfs for moulting, but obviously the more developed the rabbit is in coat and body the more chance it has of winning.

This is not a good time to show a Dwarf every week. Show it once then let it develop a bit more.

It is unusual for a young Dwarf's development of coat to be affected by showing. Even so, it is only fair to the rabbit not to overshow it.

At around eighteen to twenty week stage the rabbit will have its first full coat and should be right for the stock shows. After five month stage the rabbit is usually in the Intermediate stage as regards showing. It is too old for the young classes, not developed enough for the adult classes. This is an ideal time to commence breeding especially with does.

If your adult does have started moulting heavily they can be rested and the young maiden does will give you continuity of breeding.

This brings me to adult rabbits which moult annually and completely replace all their fur very quickly. Where the young growing rabbit slowly changes its coat, over quite a long period, the adult moult is usually a lot quicker.

All rabbits do not moult exactly the same. Usually, however, the quicker they moult the better the coat.

This is one of the most stressful periods of a rabbit's life. With my own rabbits I neither breed off them or show them when moulting. I do not handle them except for usual health checks. I do not groom them, just let the fur come away naturally. However, when they have moulted the main body of the coat and are down to the extremities, they are handled every day. This daily handling gently removes dead hair from the body and legs etc., all this aids to a good finish to the coat. The addition of a spot of glycerine on my hands, helps at this stage.

In a few weeks time the bloom is there and once the claws are clipped the rabbit is ready for showing.

I know there isn't anything mentioned in the standard about showing rabbits whilst moulting. However, there is a gentle reminder under condition. This states that the rabbit should be in good coat.

To me, it is obvious that a rabbit moulting is not "in good coat". Of course this is my opinion and interpretation only.

Now all the points of the standard have been covered, the problem is getting all or most of the standard features on one rabbit. This will always be the ultimate challenge of all Dwarf breeders.

With good selection and careful consideration of all points of the standard, there are methods we can adopt in our breeding plans to get us close to the ideal.

CHAPTER 7
The Full Picture

AFTER GOING THROUGH THE STANDARD in fine detail it is time to look at ways we can get all that is required on one rabbit. This is the ultimate challenge for all Dwarf breeders. We will always be faced with difficulties when striving to achieve the above objective. This is where all beginners struggle at first. What you need to do is get in your "mind's eye" a picture of what is required in the perfect dwarf. From a practical point of view the easiest way to achieve this is to handle as many top quality dwarfs as you can.

Stewarding at the top stock shows is the ideal way to get the qualities that are required in a good dwarf firmly fixed in your mind. Once you have got this mental picture it becomes easier to start to improve your stock.

Pair to Improve

Never breed together two rabbits just for the sake of it. What you have got to do is firmly fix in your mind why you are mating a certain two rabbits together. In my breeding plans I have two reasons why rabbits will be mated together. The first is to improve on a fault, the second is to, hopefully, breed better quality rabbits in the next generation.

Improving on faults will always be a very important consideration when selecting matings. This is particularly important to beginner breeders who are just starting to build their studs. Do not be tempted to breed together two rabbits where both carry an outstanding fault. Also never use a rabbit for breeding that carries a disqualification fault.

Sometimes beginners are so keen to see youngsters running around that little thought is used in the process of selection. In the learning period of breeding dwarf rabbits, try to learn the art of improving your stock. It will definitely pay dividends when you get more into the fascinating challenge of breeding dwarf rabbits.

Another trap beginners can fall into is when a selected pair will not mate. This can be when the doe will not accept the buck. Sometimes it is a temptation to mate it to another buck without considering the faults each rabbit can carry. In my own breeding, once I have selected a pair to be mated, I persevere with it. Usually, after a few days of trying, most rabbits will mate. If after a few days a doe will not mate I place her in a dirty hutch, where a buck has been, for twenty four hours. This usually does the trick. If it is the buck that is not interested the reverse can be done. If I intend to use a buck on a few does, he is housed near the does, or below them, about a week before I plan mating. The reverse can also apply to does; if they are not quite in mating condition they can be placed near bucks.

By moving stock around on the above lines matings are usually performed quicker. This avoids the temptation of splitting a select pair because one will not mate.

Incompatible Pairings

There is always a possibility that your chosen pair are incompatible. I have known this to occasionally happen in my stock. This is the only time I split chosen pairings but I always patiently try to get them to mate before giving up. As regards mating to improve a fault, this can become impossible in some situations. If quite a lot of your stock carry the same fault, or you feel a feature needs to be generally improved upon, an outcross is the only answer.

The second reason why I mate a selected pair together is, hopefully, to breed better quality rabbits in the next generation. To successfully deal with this interesting challenge in livestock breeding, it is important to have set plans and methods.

To improve overall quality of our dwarfs the standard has to be studied thoroughly. The best way to do this is to utilise the points allocated by the standard, in a way which can be adapted to our breeding plans. This method is called the TOTAL SCORE, and is widely used in all types of livestock breeding. Over the years I have devised different types of score systems based on the dwarf standard. I have found the following to be the best for me but there are always ways to improve any system. Every rabbit that is retained for breeding is critically assessed and is allocated points from the following table:

BODY 8	EARS 4	HEAD 5
COAT 3	COLOUR 3	CONDITION 2

This gives a total of 25 points.

I have broken this down from the standard of 100 points to make the system more manageable. The reason I score head at five points is

Top of a good Netherland Dwarf challenge class

An excellent example of an Agouti Dwarf with its Championship Certificate

Blue Otter excelling type and colour

Black showing lustrous sheen and very good type

Marten Smoke Pearl. A young adult showing good colour, just needs to fill out on head to balance

Blue showing good depth of colour and good type

The classic Red Eyed White Netherland Dwarf, showing very good side profile

Siamese Sable, best in show at the National Netherland Dwarf Club's 1996 adult stock show

because I allow one point for eyes. If a dwarf has a bold eye it gets a point, a small eye and it does not score.

Condition scores only two points because it brings the score to twenty-five. This is because I only use rabbits in excellent condition for breeding, so they all score two points.

Your main stud buck needs to score as highly as possible. Twenty to twenty-two points is a score to aim for.

Scoring for does is also very important and this is where you need to have a minimum score to be acceptable.

Let us look at an example to see how the system works.

If your buck scores twenty-two and the doe sixteen, the average for the youngsters should be nineteen.

As you can see, this score is higher than the does score. Theoretically, there should be an improvement in this generation of youngsters.

Unfortunately, in some cases, nature has a way of upsetting theory. Some youngsters will score less than nineteen but, hopefully, some will score more.

Let's get back to the minimum accepted score. The beginner breeder should set a minimum score for stock retained for breeding. This is the really important part of the system.

It is better to have a minimum for bucks and another one for does. An example could be twenty for bucks and sixteen for does.

If there is a general improvement in your stock in the first two seasons your minimum scores can be raised. This should see further improvements.

Practical Assessment

If there is not an improvement you are not scoring correctly. You have to be really critical of your stock and score every rabbit consistently and fairly.

This system cannot be relied on solely, however, as on paper two rabbits could score high points but in practice have the same fault. This is where we need to adapt the practical side of selection to the theory of the points system.

The way to do this is as follows:

Set a procedure e.g. select a pair for mating, first looking if their scores are good enough to see an improvement in the next generation. Then place the rabbits side by side for a practical assessment.

By doing this you can see immediately if they have any faults that are common to each other. If they have, their good scores will become irrelevant and the mating should be cancelled.

Whilst comparing stock together in this way much can be learned about selection of matings. For example, if the buck has very good ears it could make up for a doe that is slightly off in this department. The better quality your primary stud buck possesses the more chances of a good match when comparing stock together.

If your main stud buck fails in certain features, the practical assessment of a pairing is more difficult. Progress can still be made in this situation but you will have to rely more closely on the scoring of rabbits to be retained for breeding. This is especially important where does are being selected for the breeding programme.

It is usual for general improvement to be first noticed in the does. If this is happening you are making good progress.

Eventually the best of these does will breed a buck good enough to head the breeding programme. It is useful to keep the father of this rabbit for a while longer, perhaps until the young buck has proved himself. Sometimes getting without stock too soon can hinder the improvement process.

A careful combination of practical assessment and correct scoring of rabbits will eventually see an improvement in the stock.

After every breeding season an assessment of the stock should be made to see if your stud has improved. Are scores improving? - are better young bucks coming through? - If you can answer "yes" progress has definitely been made.

From this information you can plan next year's breeding, to hopefully make **more** progress. If you have had a bad breeding season and no improvement has been made, find out the reason. If fertility is the problem take a look at your stock management. Would an outcross be of any use? This is definitely the time of year to put things right for the next breeding season.

After a few years you should be slowly climbing to the top of your chosen colour. Staying at the top is another story. Once at the top there is only one place to go.

Maintaining standards is really difficult for the top breeders, there is always someone coming up to challenge.

This is a healthy situation and makes for a good dwarf fancy.

The competitive spirit is in all of us, please take defeats gracefully, only one rabbit can win. The next show can be different.

Having a go at the judge is no good. Most judges are not affected or impressed by such unsportsmanlike behaviour.

For a fancier to stay at the top with their respective colour for many years is a great achievement. These fanciers are few and far between and form the backbone of quality dwarfs in this country.

For fanciers climbing the ladder these are the people to approach for quality stock. Most of them thrive on competition, so will let stock go, but sometimes price is a problem.

A champion Himalayan Dwarf exhibited by Mrs Angela Saunders. A lovely Dwarf showing good deep colour on ears and smut. A typical example of a good stud maintaining quality

CHAPTER 8

Breeding, Fertility, Rearing

THE REPRODUCTIVE PROCESS is the most important aspect of any form of livestock breeding. This is especially so where the Netherland Dwarf rabbit is concerned.

Unfortunately over the years the dwarf has unfairly gained the reputation of being a bad breeder. I find the dwarf just as easy to breed as any other rabbit. The only difference is that because of its small size we only get small litters. Also, the birth size of the dwarf rabbit is a lot smaller than other breeds. This makes it more prone to chilling at its most vulnerable stage, which is the first few days of its life.

With a good common sense approach these little problems can be overcome, after all, breeding is a natural process. All we do is assist in the matter. Reproduction is just a cycle of events, starting from birth, through to adult, then back to birth again.

I will be going through the cycle using my own methods. Before doing so I think it is important that beginner breeders gain much knowledge on this subject. This can be done through books, talking to fellow breeders and generally keeping up to date with all aspects of the breeding process.

Eventually you will be able to formulate your own breeding methods but always be prepared to learn more. No one person will ever know everything about this wonderful facet of our hobby.

In my own breeding operation I have only a small stud of dwarfs, never above six of eight breeding does. In the last five years of breeding the average number of youngsters reared, to eight weeks of age, is around forty per year.

A large percentage of these go for pets. However, of the rabbits that are retained for breeding over ninety percent breed and rear successfully. Needless to say I am happy with the breeding, fertility and rearing of my stud with this ratio.

However I am always looking at ways to improve further. In the last two years I have started to breed less pets but this has caused other problems; i.e. lack of space means I have to be more selective for stock being retained for future breeding. I find this really important, especially where a concentrated inbreeding and linebreeding programme is in operation.

For me the most important part of the breeding cycle is when young adults come into breeding for the first time, so here goes. It is really important to get these first timers of to a good start, so to speak.

First, the bucks. Their part in the breeding process is of less importance than the does, but even so their needs are vital. Young bucks coming into breeding are usually rabbits that have been shown and handled a lot. All they need is a good balanced diet fed consistently.

Being handled a lot will have done them good and they should be in excellent body condition and moult free.

I always check that they have two testicles before placing a doe to them. Rabbits that are Monorchid or Cryptorchid can pass this fault to their offspring and fertility could be affected, in future generations.

At around six months old young bucks usually have a high sperm count. To these first timers I usually put a proven or older doe that is in receptive breeding condition. A young doe or a doe not quite ready could attack him, probably putting him off the breeding idea for a while. Also his prospects of showing could be spoiled by the attack.

If he mates the doe immediately he is left for a repeat performance then the doe is taken away. If she refuses to mate after a minute or two she is taken away and tried later.

The successfully mated doe is put to him again two hours later but as soon as she mates once is taken away. If an older buck is being used mating is repeated at two hourly intervals.

Sometimes the sperm count can be low from time to time in the buck, this is usually the case if the buck has not been used for a while. The continued use of the buck will result in new sperm being produced and the sperm count should rise.

Now let us look at the young maiden doe. Does have far more input into the breeding operation than the bucks, their welfare should always be well catered for.

If a doe has been reared well on a good diet and has had the opportunity of plenty of hutch exercise she should naturally come into good fertile breeding condition at around five months of age.

I always try to keep the does "lean and mean". Internal fat put on by overfeeding lowers the fertility rate.

New fanciers particularly seem to fall into a trap of overfeeding. It is a well known fact that the addition of Vitamin E supplement can aid fertility. I am a firm believer in this concept and adapt the following to my feeding routine.

Wheat is a grain high in Vitamin E content and this is always present in my staple mix in small quantities. I always keep a couple of pounds on its own however.

When the does are coming into breeding condition they are given a little extra. About a week before I plan to mate the does, a few drops of Wheatgerm oil is placed on their food each day.

Toasted brown bread also contains Vitamin E. I also add a few Sunflower seeds to their food, only small amounts are used with both. Too much wheat can lead to excessive body heat, overfeeding of Sunflower seed can cause the blood to overheat.

Once the doe is mated the above additives are cut down to once a week. The young maiden doe is always mated to a proven stud buck. The quicker the mating the better.

If she chases round she is taken away and placed back in her hutch. I never let a buck pester a maiden doe too much, she is tried every day until she mates.

If she will accept the buck without fuss she is left with him for a further mating. Two hours later she is tried again but removed as soon as she mates.

This two hour interval mating can be repeated again until she won't accept the buck any more. The day after she is tried again. If she "cries up" she is not put to the buck again. If she accepts the buck on the second day she is tried again on the third day.

The first thing I do when a doe successfully mates is to write down and record when she is due to give birth. With the rabbit we do not need a complicated Gestation Chart. I use thirty one days as the Gestation period. A rabbit mated, say on the eighteenth of a thirty one day month, will kindle on the eighteenth of the following month. If it is mated in a thirty day month, add one day on, to be due on the nineteenth. If mated in February add three days on to give birth on the twenty first.

If you work long hours but are home at weekends, mate your rabbit on a Wednesday, this way the rabbit will give birth at a weekend when you are at home.

Once the doe has been successfully mated I do not make any more checks. She is handled as little as possible, except for usual health checks.

After mating there are usually some good signs of a successful take. These are continual digging and moving of the bedding, some does soon establish a corner where they are about to kindle.

Once I see this I do not disturb the corner. If you use nest boxes place the box where she is preparing. I have used nest boxes in the past but quite a lot of my does thought they were toilets.

About a week before the doe is due the hutch is given a good clean out, not disturbing the corner she has chosen. From then until birth I literally bombard her with hay.

Sometimes the doe can make a full nest and pluck fur around the eighteen to twenty one day period, this is usually an indication of a false mating (Pseudo Pregnancy). If this occurs, destroy the nest and re-mate her to the buck at twenty one days, she should be back on cycle and have a normal pregnancy.

Sealpoint Dwarfs aged three weeks. A healthy litter content and happy, showing even litter size

During pregnancy my does are not given any extra food, just their normal diet with the inclusion of the above additives. However, in the last two weeks they probably eat a lot more hay than usual.

All this changes when the litter is born, they are then fed twice a day.

A day or so before the kindle some go off their food, this is normal and sometimes the appetite takes a couple of days to return, so do not worry about this.

As soon as the youngsters are born the doe is removed and the nest is inspected.

Dead youngsters are removed and any lethal babies are destroyed. If the nest is not very good I make it better, by banking the bedding around the nest and checking that there is enough fur lining the nest to give a good covering.

It can pay to have a bag of rabbit fur from destroyed nests in case there is a shortage. Failing this, fur can be gently plucked from the doe, this can also make the teats accessible to the youngsters.

Never panic when trying to help the doe, once you have dealt with a few kindling problems you will gain more confidence.

When you are happy with the nest and litter, gently place the doe back in her hutch. If she has been reared well she will usually accept your help, more about this when discussing rearing.

Litter size is a good indication of fertility. Four or more is excellent, three is alright, two is below average and one is poor.

I do not let the doe rear one youngster alone, in case of this situation and other eventualities I always mate at least three does at the same time. Preferably two of the does should be proven just in case the maiden has problems.

If the maiden has one youngster she is re-mated the day after kindling and the youngster is fostered to one of the other does.

When fostering I always mark the youngster so that I will know the parentage, felt tip pens are good for this but re-mark often. When fostering to another doe the recipient is removed to another hutch and the foster baby rubbed in soiled bedding in order to get the scent of the doe.

The foster baby is then placed with his new litter mates.

Before the doe is placed back she gets a small dab of Vick or similar on her nose just to dull her sense of smell for a while.

The maiden doe that has had only one youngster is watched very closely with her next two litters. If litter size does not improve she is eliminated from the breeding programme. This is one of my simple rules, there are more to follow.

When inspecting a doe that has just kindled and all youngsters are dead the doe is removed immediately, this is probably the most disappointing part of breeding especially for beginners. Unfortunately, these things happen all too often and make the best of us a little despondent. As breeders there are situations we have to learn to deal with. First I remove all youngsters and examine them for any signs of life. If there is slight movement of limbs and mouth all is not lost, I place the baby in my cupped hands and gently blow on it. If there are still signs of life it is placed down my shirt, next to my skin, making sure it can not fall out. Sometimes there can be more than one in this chilled condition, if I am not quite sure about one it is still placed down my shirt. The nest is put back to normal and the doe put back in her hutch. I then place a container on a radiator shelf, previously lined with rabbit fur, to pre-warm. While I am doing this the babies stay down my shirt, sometimes movement can be felt on your stomach. Keep calm, there is no need to rush. Next step I fill a container with warm water and each youngster is gently immersed up to the neck. This seems to stimulate them into further movement. Each, in turn, is dried with a piece of kitchen roll or soft cloth and then placed in the container on the radiator shelf. I then go back to the shed and inspect the doe again.

This is decision time. If the doe looks perky or is feeding and moving around freely I usually take a chance and put them back to her. Before doing this I make a really good job of re-making the nest also making sure the doe has a good milk supply. (If only one youngster is saved it is fostered on.) Finally a dab of Vick is placed on her nose and she is placed back to her warmed up youngsters.

The doe is watched very closely for the next few hours. If by the next day the litter is not doing well they are fostered. Once a doe has either lost a litter or had youngsters taken off her she is mated the next day. This is one of the most fertile periods, so I take advantage of it. What ever a doe does on her first birth of a litter she is forgiven but if she loses two more litters she leaves the breeding programme. These rabbits are *never* sold to other breeders. Before leaving fostering, I have to admit it is only done as a last resort. Most of my does behave very well, even the first time.

I have never contemplated hand rearing but admire people who do.

I feel young rabbits need mother's milk in the first few days of life in order to build up their immune system. Also young rabbits being reared could become imprinted to the human touch. This could cause breeding problems later.

A doe that has lost two litters, and is on her last chance, is placed close by does who are excellent breeders. Sometimes in this situation the problem doe improves her maternal habits, this has occasionally worked for me. Also when the doe loses a litter the nest is left intact for a few days. The doe can be seen brooding over the nest looking for babies. The next time she kindles she might do this with live babies.

In my strain of dwarfs a maiden doe going over her birth time is usually an indication that something is wrong. When there aren't any babies two days after the birth date, I gently massage her stomach then offer her to the buck. She usually accepts the buck and this opens her up and birth follows. In this situation babies may be stillborn or there could be only one large baby.

The doe is re-mated the day after; if the same thing happens again her days of breeding are over. If ever I am confronted with a doe with a baby that is stuck whilst giving birth, she is offered my assistance. Using warm olive oil on my fingers, I gently ease the baby away. In this situation I advise the beginner breeder to seek help from someone experienced in this little operation before attempting it themselves. The doe is re-mated as soon as everything is OK, maybe a couple of days afterwards. Again, if she gives a repeat performance next time she is out of the breeding team.

Next we come to the most frustrating part of breeding Dwarf rabbits.

You come to inspect the doe's hutch on the day she should kindle and you find nothing! The doe, in rabbit terminology, has 'missed'. Before deciding that this is the situation, examine the doe, making sure she has not just gone over her date. The word 'missed' is a broad term used by rabbit fanciers when a doe does not produce a litter after what appears to have been a successful mating.

Let us look at some reasons for this. The buck might not have been fertile at the time of mating. This could also apply to the doe. On mating the doe might not have been ovulating or the young embryos could have died part way through pregnancy, then come away and been eaten by the doe. Female rabbits have the ability to absorb the growing embryos in their wombs. This is called 'resorption' and is a trait which seems to have come from the wild rabbit. When food is scarce the wild rabbit absorbs the young and mates when food is plentiful again. In the domestic rabbit resorption occurs either from poor feeding or stress.

On re-mating the doe that has 'missed' I take more care with the mating and try to make sure it does not happen again. If a few does have 'missed' to the same buck he is test mated before being used again. Before I do this, I mate the doe to another buck which has recently sired youngsters. She is mated more often than before, say, every hour if possible. Occasionally I will hold the doe on her back for a few minutes immediately after mating. On another occasion I will place her in a travelling box for about twenty minutes. Holding a rabbit on her back gives the sperm more time to fertilize the ovulating eggs. Placing a doe in a box usually has the effect of stopping her urinating and washing the sperm away before fertilization has taken place. The continued re-mating has the effect of starting the doe to ovulate if she is not quite ready. The doe is check mated every week all through pregnancy. If after all this she misses once more she leaves the breeding team.

Back to test mating the buck. The best way to do this is to mate him to does in high breeding condition. If these fail to breed, he can be presumed to be infertile. Sometimes this can be a temporary condition and after a while fertility can return. If I have a buck that keeps losing fertility, I again remove him from the breeding team.

When quite a few does are losing litters, or missing, mice could be the problem. The need to wage war on these little devils is imperative or you will not have many more litters. I will use any means to control vermin: poison, live traps, nipper traps.

The main deterrent is to make food unavailable to the mice. My food is stored in bins with tight fitting lids, the hay is kept in a large bag and tied up. In recent years the mice have transferred their affections to my Bird Room and leave the rabbits alone.

In breeding dwarfs I have experienced all the problems outlined above. By applying these strict rules, however, the problems have become minimal. There are still a few more problems to discuss but we will come to them later.

Now let us look at the more positive side of breeding dwarfs and go to the doe that has given birth to four healthy babies buried in a deep nest of fur. This is where our hobby becomes really enjoyable and the objective is to do everything possible to make sure the youngsters are reared successfully. As I have said before, the doe is now fed twice daily so she is on double rations. Once the litter has had its initial inspection, disturbance is kept to a minimum. I just make sure the nest fur is moving whenever I attend to the doe. For the first few days I check the nest last thing at night, making sure all the youngsters are in the nest and covered up.

The youngsters grow quickly and the doe starts to produce stronger milk. She should be eating more food and drinking more water.

When the youngsters are about one week old I gradually give more food. I put a few drops of wheatgerm oil on the food, (this is for about ten days to two weeks and then finished with) - this is so the doe does not suffer from Vitamin E deficiency at a time when she is heavily feeding the babies. Vitamin E deficiency can result in a mild form of Muscular Dystrophy, so the addition of wheatgerm oil avoids this.

I like the youngsters to stay in the nest as long as possible, so only dirty parts of the hutch are cleaned out. When I clean the hutch I take the opportunity to check the youngsters and bank the nest up with the clean bedding, the doe is replaced as soon as possible.

One or two of the youngsters soon start to explore the hutch and eventually start to eat. Around the three week stage all the youngsters can be seen feeding from the pot.

A few days afterwards I see that the hutch is thoroughly cleaned out and sprayed with a strong solution of Vanodine V 18. I have used this disinfectant for a long time and find it to be excellent, it kills all mould and fungus spores and is safe to use. Rabbits can be safely replaced in the hutch immediately after use.

Before doing this I give the babies a thorough health inspection, checking eyes, vent area and limbs for deformities. From this stage food is fed virtually ad. lib. The food is placed in two pots at the front corners of the hutch; this stops the doe pushing the youngsters out of the pot and ensures all the babies get a fair share of the food.

At six weeks the litter is weaned from the doe. All should be in excellent condition and ready for quality assessment.

Any baby that has either show or breeding potential is rung and is recorded in the breeding book. Pets are not rung. All the litter is kept together for a further two weeks and fed twice a day; two pots are used as before, and watched for a few minutes to make sure they are all eating.

A Dwarf breeding doe content and happy with her rapidly growing litter

Now let us get back to the doe. She should be in good condition, even though she has just reared a litter. If she is, she is re-mated as soon as she is taken from the youngsters. She will be fertile and usually accepts the buck immediately. If down in condition, she is built up for a few days.

This breeding cycle is kept up until the doe has her next full moult. Each time she has a litter, and successfully rears it, she is mated again always checking, of course, her fitness.

These does are the backbone of my stud and I usually have about three or four at any time. They are extremely well and make up for all the problem rabbits outlined earlier. My current best breeding doe has recently reared four litters in a thirteen month period, which includes a rest for moulting.

When a doe starts to moult she is rested from breeding and placed on an adult diet, or just below, depending on her body condition. I have usually planned for this time of the year and have does coming into breeding for the first time. This gives me the chance of producing more youngsters whilst the year bred, or over, does are moulting.

Once the doe has moulted the main body of the coat she is placed on the Vitamin E additives for a week, then mated. If she misses she is put on a spartan diet, this is done only if I think she might be carrying fat. All does are individuals, some put on weight during the resting period and some do not.

The spartan diet is half normal food, fed every other day. Hay is fed as normal. This is done for about ten days and her body condition is regularly checked. The wheatgerm oil is added on the days that I feed.

If she misses again her days are numbered as a breeder. If I have room and she is a good quality doe, a last chance is given; failure means she leaves the breeding team.

Most of the does successfully rear a litter after the resting period and I do not have to resort to the diet very often. I have found that the first two years of breeding life are the best for fertility and rearing capabilities. I like to keep the stud young, especially the does, fertility is more stable in this situation.

There are of course exceptions to the rule, I have bred from does up to four years of age without any drop in fertility rate. Does like these are a bonus, especially if they are breeding good quality rabbits.

As long as there are good breeding bucks coming through the stud they are useful. Quite a lot of young does are kept from this type of rabbit. The possibility of some of them carrying the excellent breeding qualities is very high.

I rarely keep more than four bucks as breeders. One of these is the main buck and it is a must that he has PREPOTENT qualities. The rest of my hutches are used for breeding does, potential breeders and show stock.

I like to have at least three or four potential young does coming through to join the current breeding does.

The above, combined with the odd older doe, give me a wide variety of possible pairings. My rabbits breed all the year round and I try to plan things so that youngsters are coming through at regular intervals. This gives me a chance of having young breeding does joining the team at various times of the year - very important as there are stock shows held throughout the year.

This nicely brings us back to the growing litter and the work required to rear a good youngster.

Eight weeks of age is another 'sort out' time. Pets are shipped out and occasionally one of the rung youngsters joins them. This is, usually, because its 'total score' is not to my set minimum. The rabbits that are left are all housed individually and are fed as adults. This gives an adequate diet in the all important growing period. These rabbits will be either show potential or have breeding qualities.

Some youngsters possess both ideals and this is a bonus, especially in a small stud. These are handled every day, the show prospects taking priority. All these rabbits will sit and pose, naturally, for this is part of my selection. I find that this handling really worthwhile and it is a characteristic of the breed that can become fixed in your stock. It also improves the posture and bad habits can be corrected, like parting the ears, dipping their heads down and rising up.

After a while most rabbits learn what is required and seem to enjoy the little handling sessions. I look for youngsters that set themselves very quickly and retain their posture. When they are doing this consistently I step well away from them in the hope that they will keep position for a while. During handling I occasionally turn them up and inspect their teeth and underparts. All this gets them used to the rigours of the show bench.

The potential breeders are also handled daily, if possible, especially the does. Their posing capabilities are not as important, but with gentle handling they become more confident in me, also they are less stressful and seem to come on better. This confidence between rabbit and handler really pays dividends later when you have to inspect litters etc.

I find some young rabbits find it difficult to accept life on their own, these are watched very closely. If they become too stressed they are prone to scour and this can lead to a mild or violent bout of Enteritis.

Immediately I find this condition steps are taken to try and alleviate the symptoms. The hutch is thoroughly cleaned out and a small amount of food, with half a Weetabix on top, is placed at the front of the cage. Before placing the rabbit back it is gently cleaned up ensuring that the vent area is clear. A small amount of live yogurt is hand fed to the rabbit. Your Vet. can supply a little syringe which is ideal for any form of forced mouth feeding.

Once the treatment is completed the rabbit can be placed back in the cage and quietly observed. Treatment is continued twice a day for the next few days even when the scouring stops. If the rabbit slowly starts to eat it can be encouraged with a little more Weetabix.

When improvement is seen a small amount of hay is given. At the next feeding time all hay not eaten is removed and replaced with fresh. Until the rabbit is making a good recovery the removal of the hay is continued every day.

Sometimes the rabbit may only be eating a little, then a small amount of Minadex is placed in the drinker. If the rabbit does not make a full recovery and fails to get back to good body condition, it is not good enough for breeding. Bad 'doers' can play no part in my breeding programme. I will not risk weakness being passed on to future generations.

With good management, and a little luck, the rabbits will slowly progress to breeding age. We have come full circle and another generation of Dwarfs is almost with us. In the next chapter I consider Inbreeding and Linebreeding, always a controversial subject but if it is to be applied with any success, rabbits that are fertile and breed well, are essential requirements.

CHAPTER 9

Linebreeding and Inbreeding

FOR MANY YEARS the subject of inbreeding has always been prone to much controversy. Some people think it is immoral for related stock to be bred together. Others think it could be a dangerous practice. Usually it is the people who do not fully understand the concept of inbreeding that are against its usefulness in livestock breeding.

Whilst it is definitely immoral for human relatives to be bred together, the truth is the animal kingdom does not have moral standards. As for inbreeding being dangerous, it is up to the breeder not to allow it to be so. More about this later.

Since a teenager I have used the technique of inbreeding as a method of improving quality in rabbits. I have also successfully bred dogs, pigeons and canaries following selective inbreeding and linebreeding programmes. By far the most difficult problems I have come across have been with the Netherland Dwarf Rabbit. Learning from these difficulties and mistakes has made me more confident of successfully improving a stud of dwarf rabbits by the careful blending of inbreeding, linebreeding and outcrossing.

It is the aim of this chapter to help the beginner breeder, from a practical point of view, towards achieving the above. As for the theory side of the subject, my advice, as on other topics, is to learn as much as possible. Unfortunately I have always found that nature has a way of upsetting theory and that practical experience is the only way to progress. Before getting down to the subject of inbreeding in detail, a little background information may be useful.

Two of the most important points to come from Charles Darwin's "Origin of the Species" are, natural selection and survival of the fittest. Animals in the wild, especially herding type species, naturally select their own mates. Also the most dominant males are usually the fittest and are the ones responsible for siring the most offspring. Both these situations give rise to natural inbreeding. The reason for its success rate is because only the fittest animals are responsible for the majority of young that are bred in every generation. Any weaknesses that occur naturally die out and the fittest animals perpetuate the species.

When we look at the domestic breeding of livestock we the breeders are responsible for selection of suitable mates. This artificial selection of mates, so to speak, is only as good as our ability to select chosen pairs that will successfully improve our stock. In this situation we cannot blame the animals for breeding poor stock. We covered 'selection of stock for breeding' earlier in the book but as far as inbreeding is concerned care with selection is vital to success. As regards fitness of animals used for breeding, again the responsibility lies with the breeder and, hopefully, his good stock management. With the fitness required for inbreeding I take into consideration the fertility, breeding and rearing capabilities of the dwarf.

Quite a few years ago I made the mistake of trying to inbreed with dwarfs that had poor fertility. The stock was of excellent quality but I could not breed enough rabbits to successfully improve the stud. This poor fertility became fixed in the rabbits and eventually resulted in my having to start all over again. This is why I have set strict rules with this aspect of stock selection so that it will not happen again.

One of the relevant phrases from Mendel's 'Laws of Inheritance' is "like breeds like". In theory I fully agree with this but from a practical point of view various things happen in breeding that contradict it. The main one is the 'Mutation Gene' for dwarfism which was covered in chapter 5, Early Creations.

It plays an important part with inbreeding so a recap will not go amiss.

The show type dwarf (Dw dw) is the one we would hope to breed like to like. Unfortunately from this pairing we also get the pet/breeder type (dw/dw) which is very unlike the show type we are aiming for. As far as inbreeding is concerned a doe from this pet/breeder type can be very useful, more about the ugly doe later.

It is also more difficult for 'like breeding like' to work by continued outbreeding. This type of breeding is where unrelated animals are bred together. In this situation different genetical makeups come together. Some of these inherited genes can carry impurities and the result is usually a wide variety of types being bred.

The bonus with this system is that the majority of stock bred is extremely healthy, due to hybrid vigour.

With dwarfs, however, continued outbreeding makes it very difficult to progress and get some sort of uniformity in the stud. Occasionally two rabbits can knit together and breed rabbits of similar quality to themselves. If the beginner breeder starts of with unrelated stock it is still possible to progress. The first pairings can be used to learn the art of selecting future breeding stock. When a certain pair knit together and improved stock are bred this could be the platform to start a successful inbreeding programme. If the newcomer has bought stock that is related he has moved another step up the ladder. In this situation, as I have said before, it is better to follow the advice of the person who supplied the stock.

Well we have nicely reached the stage of inbreeding, an interesting and rewarding part of breeding Netherland Dwarf Rabbits.

The first point to get over is that inbreeding does not have any magical qualities. Good rabbits will never be bred from mediocre ones unless there are outstanding qualities back in the pedigree. The old saying "you can't breed a racehorse out of two circus ponies" is really true. It is a must to have as good a quality as possible to start off with and then gradually improve and maintain that quality.

When an inbreeding programme has been started rabbits start to come through the stud that carry the same or similar genes. In this situation there is more uniformity present in the rabbits. As well as this, occurring recessive faults will start to appear more frequently than when outbreeding was practiced. It is important to eradicate these faults as soon as they appear.

A good example of a recessive fault is overgrown teeth. For this to appear in the stock both parents have to carry the recessive gene. When outbreeding, this gene can be hidden because, probably, less animals carry it. When animals are inbred, however, more rabbits will come through carrying the recessive faulty gene. By removing stock that carries any of these recessive faults from the programme, improved genetic purity will start to take place.

On the positive side good traits, like good ears and heads, can become fixed. The important point is to eliminate the bad faults and breed in the good traits.

Inbreeding is the breeding together of closely related animals. Two examples would be brother to sister and half brother to half sister. It is the quickest way to fix both good and bad points, so careful assessment of stock bred from these pairings is essential.

Linebreeding is a kind of inbreeding but rabbits used are usually more distantly related. Examples would be grandfather to granddaughter or grandmother to grandson. Successful linebreeding usually occurs when one rabbit is used pretty heavily in the programme. Every rabbit bred after a few generations has the original rabbit as its common ancestor. If the original animal is of very good quality the likelihood of similar quality rabbits being bred, as the line develops, is very high.

A good way to start a new line off is a father to daughter pairing. Next step is to mate the resultant granddaughter back to the original buck and so on.

Progressing from this, different lines can be set up and kept apart until there is a need to cross over. This is usually when one of the lines is lacking in a feature the other possesses.

In my own breeding programme I use both inbreeding and linebreeding matings. I never breed brother to sister together, my favourite pairing is half brother to half sister, preferably out of the same buck. The buck used to produce these two rabbits is usually a few generations older and also the head of a line. The doe bred from the half brother/half sister mating is usually mated to a buck which is the head of another line.

I am constantly on the lookout for a young buck coming through that is good enough to head up a line. A useful mate for this new buck is an older doe, preferably a couple of generations older. I mentioned, briefly, this type of doe in the last chapter on breeding. Occasionally these does are used for linebreeding on the doe side of the pedigree. This is especially so if she is consistently breeding good quality youngsters.

Mother/son or Grandmother/grandson are ideal pairings for this type of doe. By the above selection of pairings I am usually mating young does to older bucks and vice versa.

I have found this blend of inbreeding/linebreeding to really work for me. However, matings are not just made because they look good on paper. A typical mating will be planned as follows.

The total scores are taken of both rabbits and considered. Then the rabbits are placed side by side and a full practical assessment made of the prospective pair. Finally both pedigrees are looked at closely to see how they are related. If all is well, the mating takes place.

The 'Ugly' doe plays a big part in my inbreeding programme but she is subject to certain rules. I find these does are usually very fertile and because of their size are capable of rearing larger litters, usually of uniform size, depending on which buck they are mated to. The ugly doe is not given a total score but it is important that both her parents have good total scores. These will be show-type dwarfs and the chances of the ugly doe carrying this trait is high. The ugly doe is usually mated to the best, or primary, stud buck. Its father would be ideal. No ugly does are kept from this mating. Future ugly does, kept for breeding, must come from the best pairings of show type specimens.

By following these simple rules good quality in the breeding does is maintained and only one or two ugly does are used in the breeding programme.

I do not get despondent when faulty genes occur through inbreeding. The following are a few of the faults I have come across: overgrown teeth, bent front legs, blind eyes, persistent running eyes and very weak youngsters. It is not only important to eliminate these faulty rabbits from the stud but to also remove rabbits that are carriers of these recessive faults. Selective test matings can be used to find these culprits. Although time may be lost it is the only effective way of eradicating these recessive faults.

By not doing the above I once completely ruined a stud of excellent Marten Sables. The problem was bent legs. Some very good dwarfs were being bred but more and more rabbits were coming through with the bent leg problem. Eventually a large percentage of the dwarfs I was breeding became carriers of this fault. I had fixed this fault in my stud. All the rabbits had to be disposed of, another lesson learned and a costly one as well. So at the first sign of any of the above faults, get to the root of the problem and sort it out.

I find it important to keep the stud young in my inbreeding programme. Exceptions to this are bucks at the head of a line and the occasional older doe mentioned previously. A succession of young does coming through the stud gives a wide range of pairings to choose from. This is really important in a small stud.

Once an inbreeding programme has become established and good quality stock is coming through with regularity, the likelihood of a rabbit with prepotent qualities being bred is possible.

I have mentioned prepotency earlier in the book but if a prepotent rabbit turns up in your breeding it gives your stud a new dimension. A buck with this quality will have great influence on the quality of the stud whichever doe he is mated to. The majority of the progeny he breeds will be better than himself. The result will be a rapid improvement of the stud and a good opportunity to maintain this improvement on a long term basis.

At this level a good strain of dwarfs will have developed. There will be a striking resemblance between each rabbit, all possessing a close genetic likeness. Their good qualities will be fixed and each will have the ability to transmit these characteristics to their descendants. In this type of strain sometimes two individuals, of no special value in themselves, can produce young of outstanding quality far superior to themselves. A popular phrase for this is 'nicking' and when it occurs it is a real bonus.

Although all seems to be going well, even in the above situation, sooner or later an outcross will be required.

Continuous inbreeding and linebreeding can lower the vigour in the animals being bred. If this is allowed to continue the stud could stagnate and maintenance of quality would become more difficult. At the level of the strain mentioned above an outcross would create hybrid vigour and gradually as pairings progressed all the stud would benefit from it.

I firmly believe that outcrossing is the most important part of the inbreeding operation. As well as providing hybrid vigour, outcrosses can be used to generally improve quality and also to eradicate certain faults.

Before discussing these it is necessary to look at how the outcross can initially effect the stud. The term outcrossing means bringing in unrelated stock. In this situation similar things happen as when the inbreeding programme was first started. The unrelated rabbit could bring in undesirable faults and faulty recessive genes.

Progeny from the first mating have to be watched very closely. Rabbits that are bred showing the undesirable traits need to be removed from the breeding team. Again, as with the setting up of the original inbreeding, any carriers of faulty genes that are found also need to be eliminated. The end product will be the eventual eradication of the faulty genes.

To minimise the effect of the above it is better to bring in a doe as the outcross. The doe could be mated to your primary stud buck and does from the mating taken back to him. If all is going well the next generation of youngsters could be bred to other members of the stud. This gradual blending of the outcross is usually the key to its success.

Where improvement of overall quality is concerned a buck may be the best option for the outcross. An example of this could be when a beginner breeder, who has started an inbreeding programme, finds that his overall quality of stock needs improving. The best way to progress is to either buy an outstanding buck or to get a mating with your best doe to such an animal.

Never be afraid to ask the owner to show you its parents or anything it has bred. From such a mating or rabbit two lines can be set up on both sides of the pedigree. If the outcross was a mating a daughter will have to go back to the same buck. It is worth paying for this service as general improvement should follow. Once established, inbreeding can continue with (hopefully) better quality stock.

An outcross to eradicate a fault is a different matter. If the fault is general to all the stud it could take a few generations of careful breeding to sort it out. A way forward would be to get an outcross doe that excels in the department lacking. This is better mated to a buck in your stud that is least affected by the general fault. If it is ears, for instance, it will be the buck which has the best ears. The original outcrossed litter may not show immediate improvement. Linebreeding to either one side or the other should achieve the desired result after a few generations. Once an improvement has been made further inbreeding should fix the feature.

Sometimes a beginner can benefit by obtaining the outcross from a similar strain to his own, by going to a breeder who has got his stock from the same breeder as he has. In this way there is a better chance of the outcross working. This term is described as a distant outcross mating that usually immediately blends with the stock. This distant type outcross could prove worthwhile to both breeders of the same strain and is well worth a try.

My own outcrosses are usually of dual purpose. I occasionally bring

Agouti into the black stud to keep base colour sound. At the same time I get the bonus of hybrid vigour. I usually buy a young doe about ten weeks old, with good type. This way the young rabbit gets used to my management routine and is well settled by mating time. A buck bred from the outcross is only used if it is outstanding and even then in a limited way. This only happens if the outcross has knit well.

This brings me to another mistake I made quite a few years ago. I bred a really outstanding buck from an outcross mating; when he was of breeding age he was so good I mated him to every doe in the place. In three of the litters overgrown teeth were present. In fact, one litter all had bad teeth (overgrown). The problem was soon sorted out at the expense of a little time lost and not as many good youngsters coming through.

I learned two very important lessons from this experience: first, to use a buck very steadily in future. The second, more important, needs explaining. It was obvious that the buck was a carrier of the recessive fault. In the process he found three does that were carrying the faulty gene. I knew the fault was present in the stud as I had the occasional teeth problem. The conclusion is that it is not always necessary to get with out every carrier of a recessive fault. If one or two carriers are known they can be useful in finding others and therefore keeping on top of the problem.

By test mating you start to understand your stock more fully. Knowing your stock is definitely a key to success with inbreeding. Another way I get an outcross into my stud is to loan out one of my bucks. This is done on the understanding that I get a young doe from him, in return for providing the loan. In this way I am helping a fellow breeder to get going and get a young doe back with fifty percent of my bloodline.

I have always liked to work with a small stud, simply because I can keep track of everything easily. In this respect I usually use an outcross every four or five generations, normally this is every three years. We are lucky breeding dwarfs as it is possible to have two generations in one year. Rabbits from my stud, from early in the year, will be producing youngsters by August. Dwarfs from these will be breeding at the beginning of next year. Another advantage of a small stud is that it is easier to keep accurate records. This is a must in a selective inbreeding and linebreeding programme.

CHAPTER 10
Record Keeping

THE KEEPING OF ACCURATE RECORDS plays a major part in successfully building a good stud of Netherland Dwarf rabbits. This is especially so when we turn our attention to breeding and selection of matings which, hopefully, will result in improving our stock.

There are many different ways of keeping records and it is usually better for the owner to use a system he is comfortable with. Such systems include hutch record cards, a breeding register or maybe a computer programme. Many fanciers in recent years have adopted the computer programme as a successful way of keeping records. For anyone who has a little knowledge of the computer an excellent record system can easily be set up.

Before going any further let us look at the basic requirements needed in order to set up a good system. First, the records should be kept simple and easy to follow. Second, records should give as much information as possible in all aspects of the breeding programme. Thirdly, perhaps more important, all entries should be made consistently and follow a pattern you are happy with.

At this point I will go through my own record system as some of it may be of help to the beginner breeder. I have used this system for many years and have found it a valuable part of the operation. I keep two books, a stud book for bucks and a breeding book for does. A typical entry in the breeding book would be as follows:

54 BLACK DOE   94 X 09100
Born   29-3-'94
Sire   Black Boy (Black)
Dam   48 (Agouti)
Date 5 months   16-8-94
Total Score   18.
General comments   Good all round, for type. Carries a few white
                        hairs in chest.
Mated   to Black Boy 26-8-94
Date due   26-9-94 (missed) presumed overweight, put on spartan
                diet.

Re-mated   Black Boy 5-10-94
Date due   5-11-94
                    Kindle to date, four young, all even size and O.K.
Date 6 weeks   24-12-94
                    Three rung, all blacks. 94X 14678, 94X 14688, 94X
                    14679 plus one pet.
                    Doe a little down in condition, rested for a few days.
Mated   to Blackjet 1-2-95
Date due   4-3-95
                    Kindle to date, five, all blacks. O.K., an even litter
                    size.
Date 6 weeks   15-4-95
                    Two rung, 95X 06570, 95X 06572, and three for pets.

As can be seen this is a record of a maiden doe, joining the breeding team in August 1994. I give all the breeding does a number, starting at one, continuing to one hundred and then starting again at number one. Whilst I have been breeding dwarfs I have gone from one to one hundred a few times. This number, as well as going in the breeding book, is placed on the doe's hutch using adhesive labels. The labels are handy for other things as well, more about this later. If the doe above (54) was the last entry in the breeding book the next doe to join the breeding team would be (55) and so on. The book I use is an ordinary small hard back note book, this is a handy size and good enough for the system.

The entry I have described is made out on a double sheet across the book. 'Date of birth' is an obvious entry and I always like to record the colour of the sire and dam. This is very useful when different compatible colours are being bred together. It helps to give information as to what colour you will get from future matings.

'Date when the rabbit is five months' tells me, approximately, when I expect her to come into breeding condition. I use five calendar months for this period and find that most of my does are ready for this time. It is useful to write this date on her hutch, it reminds me to watch her activities around this time.

The entry for 'Total score' goes on all breeding does records, except for the 'ugly' doe. We covered Total Score in a previous chapter. My minimum total score for does is sixteen.

I find the general comments entry to be very important as it gives an immediate reminder of any faults a particular rabbit may carry. This can help avoid putting two rabbits together with the same fault. As the breeding doe develops into the stud, additional comments can be added. These could be, for instance, 'good mother', 'good feeder' etc. This information is useful if you need to foster youngsters. Mating such a doe at the same time as a maiden doe could be a bonus in case of trouble. As can be seen the doe in the example got off to a bad start. I originally put this down to her being a greedy feeder, hence the diet. The buck I mated her to, however, had not mated a doe since his resting period for moult, the record since seems to indicate that the buck lost his fertility for a while after his moult. This information was confirmed after I looked at the stud book. Another doe missed to him around the same time. As can be seen, from the record, her breeding form has improved and she is mated again and looks like becoming a prolific breeder.

'Date six weeks' is another important entry. This is the time I sort my youngsters out. Any stock with breeding potential is rung and entered in the book. It is from this source that, eventually, a breeding rabbit's details can be checked. The buck Black Boy is now back to its full fertility and has sired quite a few young so far this season.

This brings us to bucks and the stud book. Again a similar hard backed book is used but it is set out differently. A buck is only entered in the stud book if I consider he has breeding potential. He is given a name which is entered both in the stud book and on his cage. The reason I name bucks, and not does, is simple. I only use a few bucks so finding names is relatively easy. With the does it is different, many more does are used and there are always young does that join the team and it is more simple to give them numbers. However I have, on occasion, given some does names, especially when they miss or lose litters etc., unfortunately these cannot be put into print!

A typical entry in the stud book for bucks would be as follows;

BLACK JET   93X 11686
Sire   Little Blackjack
                   1992 Bradford winner.
Dam   (39)   Black (out of Black Diamond)
Total Score   22

General comments   Well balanced, small and compact. Very quick
stud (needs test mating)

LATE 1994 and 1995 BREEDING

DOE SERVED	NO IN LITTER	STOCK RETAINED + RING NUMBERS
56	3	94X 14685 + 94X 14682
54	3	95X 06570 + 95X 06572
60	4	
61	3	

Black Jet came into the programme at the back end of 1993. He
soon made his mark and bred two good dwarfs to the first two does he
was mated to.

The initial format in the stud book is similar to the breeding book.
Information on sire and dam are the first entries on the record. The
reason I entered 'out of Black Diamond' is a gentle reminder to me.
This rabbit was an excellent stud buck with prepotent qualities, so I
always have a constant reminder of what he has sired.

Again the entry Total score is very important. My minimum for stud
bucks is twenty.

General comments. Again another important entry. The term "very
quick stud" means he mates the does quickly and does not play about.

Late 1994 and 1995 needs a little explaining. When a buck has finished
his moult I make a new entry into the stud book. This roughly covers
a twelve month period until the rabbit moults again. The reason I do
this is to record the buck's performance over this period. If his record
is good he is retained the following year when, hopefully, more young
does will be available as mates for him.

From this point on I make a chart in the stud book. This is because
the buck will probably be mated to a few does within a short period of
time. All the relevant details cannot be filled in at once, so the chart
makes it easier.

The column 'DOE SERVED' gives a quick indication as to which
does in the stud he has been mated to.

'NUMBER IN LITTER' give a good yardstick as to the buck's
fertility. As can be seen from this entry fertility is very good.

Entry in the last column 'STOCK RETAINED + RING

NUMBERS' is, perhaps, the most important entry of all. The more ring numbers that are in this column the better the quality of the stud buck. Black Jet is developing into a very good stud buck, in fact in the next twelve months he may become the primary stud buck.

This is why I have written "needs test mating" in the general comments. I think he may possess Prepotent qualities, there are quite a few things pointing to this.

First, he is from a line that has produced this quality before. Secondly, he has produced good quality young to a few different does. Does sixty and sixty one are maiden does on first litters. The youngsters are, at present, about five weeks old, with good quality in both litters.

Thirdly, two of the does that have had good youngsters to him are from different lines and are quite distantly related to him. Test mating during the current breeding season will give me more information still as to his prepotency.

I will try two things out, one is a mating to an 'ugly' doe and the other is a mating to a doe that does not suit him. If good quality rabbits come from both matings he will have proved his prepotency. If this is so he will become the primary stud buck.

At this point it may be useful to add that I have better quality bucks in the shed than Black Jet, he has only been shown as a youngster as he is too small to compete in a good class of adults. His qualities as a stud buck, however, are very good. In fact he has bred better rabbits than himself for show quality. All this information points to the possibility of him being prepotent and all will be revealed within the next twelve months.

At this point I must stress that the mating just mentioned, i.e. to a doe that does not suit, is only done as part of the testing process. If it back fires and poor quality youngsters are produced all that it does is prove a point.

Where the Breeding book and Stud book becomes really useful is when a mating is being selected. The two books are placed side by side and opened at their respective places. Inside a few minutes the pedigrees of both buck and doe can be checked as to their suitability as a mating. I have a tendency to look for prominent bucks figuring on both sides of the pedigree. These are sometimes the best matings, although practical assessment is taken into consideration also. As well as the two books I also have a large calendar pinned up in a prominent place in the shed. All kindling dates are entered as well as in Breeding book. At a glance I know which does are due to kindle so that I can supply them with extra hay, well before the birth date.

The adhesive labels I mentioned earlier are really useful as reminders. An example would be when a litter is taken from the doe and placed in a cage of their own.

I write on the label the date when they are eight weeks old and which doe they came from. I trust nothing to memory; it does not matter how many labels are on the cages, it is better than forgetting something important.

Well, that is my record system but I would advise beginners to look at ways of improving any system that is adopted. If a system is working well it gives the fancier peace of mind.

CHAPTER 11
Health Problems

ONCE WE HAVE STARTED TO BUILD A GOOD STUD of dwarfs it is more important than ever to keep them fit and healthy. Unfortunately, no matter how well we care for our stock, health problems can be expected to crop up from time to time.

It is better to adopt the attitude of "prevention is better than cure". As I have said previously, observation of your stock is very important.

Every rabbit in my stud is given a full health check every week. Also, after every feeding I spend ten minutes watching my stock, looking for any problems etc.

It is not my intention to discuss the major diseases. More often than not vaccination and veterinary treatment is a must in these situations.

Whilst on the subject of veterinary treatment I am afraid I belong to the old school of livestock breeders: I use veterinary help only if it is absolutely necessary, or if I need information.

I am a little clinical with livestock and usually resort to the kill or cure method.

I am not advocating that beginners adopt my principles. My advice is to find a vet who really understands rabbits and small livestock.

More importantly, it is better to find out as much as possible about rabbit ailments yourself. There are still fanciers around who have a great wealth of knowledge on this subject. Get to know them, especially the ones who live nearby.

The largest percentage of rabbit deaths in dwarfs are by the result of diarrhoea, scours and enteritis, so I will deal with these first.

I touched on this subject in an earlier chapter but as it causes so many problems we will look at it again in more detail.

Nearly every rabbit will get some form of diarrhoea or scours in its lifetime. Mild forms are easy to treat if caught early enough. These mild forms are usually caused by a change in feed, greedy feeding or inflammation of the caecum or hind gut. The following can usually sort the problem out.

Add few drops of Kaolin and Morphine in the drinking water or if the rabbit will take greens, offer it a few raspberry or strawberry leaves.

If it doesn't, a sprinkling of arrowroot on the food usually has the affect of tightening the bowels.

Scours usually affects young rabbits from the weaning stage onwards. Upset in the feeding routine can be the cause. Eating too many greens or overeating on early season hay, as well as stress can also cause scours.

A good remedy is live yogurt.

Rabbits recovering from scours or diarrhoea need a good lining on their stomachs so a sprinkling of pinhead oatmeal or porridge oats on the food will help in this situation.

The different types of enteritis, leading up to mucoid enteritis, provide us with real problems when rearing young rabbits.

Mild types of enteritis can be treated in a similar way to scours; however, if the rabbit recovers it is important to give some form of vitamin supplement to aid recovery and bring the appetite back to normal.

I find Minadex ideal for this situation and the rabbits take to it readily.

The more violent types of enteritis such as Mucoid Enteritis are killers. This type knocks the rabbit for six and it could be dead inside twenty four hours.

Sure signs of the disease are very soft droppings and in extreme cases a jelly like substance is present. There is a foul smell present and often the rabbit is hunched up and grinding its teeth.

If action is taken quickly the rabbit can be saved but all too often death occurs.

Preventative measures can be taken to avoid this. The drinking water can be medicated with Embazin or Sulphaquin Oxaline. This is usually done about three times per year - for instance, March, July and October.

About two years ago I lost quite a few rabbits from the weaning stage onwards, so I decided I would try to resolve the situation.

In my canary management I use Probiotics both before and during the breeding season. I have used this system for a few years with great success, so I decided to experiment on the rabbits. After all, nothing would be lost and, hopefully, something gained.

Unlike antibiotics, Probiotics eradicate the unfriendly bacteria and help to promote friendly ones. In this situation the digestive system is more able to fight off bugs and stomach upsets, etc. This is the simplest way I can explain how Probiotics work.

I decided to treat rabbits at eight weeks old until four months old. The product I use is Entrodex.

The live yogurt, mentioned previously is a natural probiotic but products such as Entrodex act in a more controlled way.

My method of administering Entrodex is to add it, on the tip of a teaspoon, into a small hamster drinker full of water. I give this for four days and then for two days just plain water. Rabbits readily accept it and after a few days have an increase in appetite.

Entrodex contains vitamins and minerals also electrolytes essential to good health. Electrolytes contain vital salts which are lost from the body when a rabbit is suffering from diarrhoea or scours.

In the past year I have not lost one rabbit to scours or enteritis, so probiotics will continue to be used in my management routine. I will probably use it more extensively on rabbits that are under the weather or suffering from any type of fatigue e.g. after weaning a litter or during a heavy moult.

Hutch burn and vent disease have caused a lot of problems in dwarf breeding in the last few years. Hutch burn is relatively easy to cure and can be cleared up in a few days. Milopen or Streptopen cream obtained from your vet will do the trick. Both are penicillin based usually used on cows with milking problems. Vent disease is more serious and if it gets a good hold it is difficult to eradicate.

Mild cases can be cured by Streptopen, more acute cases are difficult to eradicate totally. Sometimes the disease will clear up, to reappear later.

In some really bad cases only a course of injections will sort it out.

I feel that these problems can be inherited in the stud, so I will not use rabbits with vent disease in my breeding programme.

In my opinion, when inbreeding and line breeding such problems can be fixed in the stock.

The final problem I will deal with around the vent area is red water. This is usually caused by cold or damp affecting the function of the kidneys; also overeating of green food can be the cause.

The rabbit is best placed in a warm hutch with an abundance of clean shavings. Give the rabbit a solution of barley water to drink for about two days. If this fails, two or three drops of sweep spirit of nitre should be given in the drinker for a further three days. If this problem occurs frequently, especially if more than one rabbit is involved, try a different type of bedding or look at a change in diet.

Sneezing in the rabbit shed always sends a cold shiver down my spine. Immediately you find a rabbit sneezing it needs to be placed in a clean hutch, well away from the rest of the stock.

A block of hutches well away from the rabbitry can prove to be a good investment when isolation is required to prevent the problem spreading.

Now check the rabbit. Look to see if there is a foreign body in the nostril that could be causing the problem. If this is not the case, more observation is required over the next few days. As long as it is away from other rabbits time is not important. Check the nose for a mucous discharge after sneezing.

Another indication that the nose is discharging is that the inside of the front legs are really wet. A simple cold treatment might be effective. If the rabbit looks otherwise healthy give it the cold cure in its drinker. There are many types of cold cure on the market for humans - try one of these, it could work. A liquid cure would be the best with just a small amount in the drinker.

Again, observation is the key. Is the sneezing getting better or worse? If more rabbits are starting to sneeze the problem is more serious. If the suspect rabbit seems to be better, keep it outside for a week before placing it back in the shed to ensure the sneezing has stopped completely. If the sneezing is worse and the mucous discharge is thicker, you could be looking at the possibility of Snuffles. This is a killer and also highly contagious. All rabbits that have the symptoms need to be destroyed. I know this sounds drastic but rabbits are seldom cured from this disease. The really important thing is if the isolation method has been in operation, less rabbits will be involved. In this situation the importance of these isolation methods cannot be stressed too much.

By far the best preventative for all snuffles, colds and respiratory type infections is the provision of good ventilation in the rabbitry. Providing as much ventilation as possible is very important, taking as much care not to provide draughts at the same time. This is especially so in wet and wintry weather.

In my own rabbit shed all hutches are 18 inches above floor level, this benefits me in two ways. Not having to bend down too much helps my arthritic condition, but the main reason is for ventilation. On the more sheltered side of my rabbit shed the bottom 18 inches has a full mesh front running the full length of the shed. The side of my shed is open at the back of the mesh and is situated next to my birdroom, and

this protects the shed from the wind and from draughts. At both ends of my shed a small section near the roof is also meshed, another is in the door with the top quarter being meshed. A free flow of air is present at all times.

The disadvantage is that in winter it is very cold, but it is never draughty.

This type of ventilation also removes any ammonia fumes that have a tendency to build up in most rabbitries, besides being rather smelly ammonia can affect the rabbits' respiratory systems. Weaker rabbits can succumb to respiratory problems. This is most likely to happen when the rabbitry is overcrowded, so it is better to avoid overcrowding and to provide good ventilation.

A typical rabbitry with a fancier busily attending to the stock. Please note the room between both sides of stock cages. It is easy to tend to stock and allows good ventilation in the shed. Also, there is adequate room for storage

For ventilation purposes and also another reason that I will discuss later, it is important that the beginner really studies where is the best place to site the rabbitry.

Ideally it should be in the most sheltered spot in the garden, one where direct sunshine does not reach through the windows. Sun can be a problem in rabbit sheds, more on this later.

If the shed is already erected in an unsuitable place, all is not lost. To improve ventilation in a shed in the open a series of holes can be drilled in the floor with fine mesh placed over them; the larger the shed the more holes can be drilled. Perhaps a small surround could be placed around this vent to limit shavings and bedding blocking this opening. This should provide a good intake of fresh air into the rabbitry.

An outlet for stale air could be provided by fitting a louvred section in the wall of the shed, as high as possible. Ventilation can be improved further by the addition of an extractor fan, especially valuable in hot weather and it can be used as required.

Depending on the size of the shed, ventilation and air quality could be improved by the use of an Ioniser. This is also of value to a breeder who is allergic to dust etc. or suffers from asthma. The Ioniser controls the negative ions in the air and keeps dust particles to a minimum helping to purify the air. Improving ventilation and ensuring that the air is pure all contribute to the prevention of respiratory and cold problems.

Earlier in the book I covered eye problems; good ventilation and avoidance of draughts can also help to prevent or limit eye troubles in the stock.

Next we move to feet problems. Sore hocks can affect some strains of dwarf. Usually the finer the coat, the more they are suspect to this trouble. Sometimes it is the back feet only that is affected. If the skin is broken the foot should be gently bathed in warm salt water and thoroughly dried then an antiseptic cream applied. I have used Cetavlex with success.

The rabbit hutch should have a generous covering of clean white shavings; sometimes with acute cases it is a good idea to put a layer of straw over the shavings. Regular cutting of the rabbit's claws can help to minimise the problem of sore hocks. The overlength claw has the effect of putting extra pressure on the hock part of the foot.

If the infection will not clear up and more fur is coming off the foot Mange Mite could be the problem. The only way to cure this is to remove the parasite. Alugan, which is a dip, can be obtained from the vet. This involves regular dipping of the rabbit's feet in the solution in order to eradicate the mite. Once all the mange has been cleared the fur will grow back to normal.

From time to time mites and fleas can appear on the coat of an otherwise healthy rabbit. These can, sometimes, be picked up at shows or can be airborne, usually in the summer, and enter the rabbitry this way. This is a simple problem to sort out. I use a product called Dynamite made by Stock Nutrition. I have used this in the birdroom since it first came out and find it excellent. It was only by chance that I started to use it on the rabbits. After returning home from a show, I noticed fleas on one of the rabbits, and as I always have a solution of Dynamite made up in a spray, I decided to give the rabbit a quick spray. Inside a few hours there was not a sign of fleas. The product is a blend of extract of herbs and is perfectly safe to use. It does not harm the coat, in fact it can improve the coat. As a precaution I always spray the show rabbits in the summer show season and none has ever come home again with fleas.

The moult, although not a health problem, can cause stress even in a healthy rabbit. Young rabbits which change their coat slowly are less affected by the moult than adults. Even so, a young rabbit in heavy moult needs close observation especially ensuring that it is eating and drinking normally. It is not advised to show a young rabbit in this heavy moult, maybe wait a week or two until there is only a slight moult present.

Young stock shows pose a problem as sometimes a rabbit can be the right age for a particular class, but be in a heavy moult. In this situation it is better to take another youngster with a slight moult, as all young rabbits are in some stage of moulting throughout the growing stage and the rabbit with the least moult has a better chance of being placed. Most judges will not place a heavily moulting youngster, so really you are usually wasting your time and more important still, could ruin the rabbit.

Moulting in the adult is a little different. Most adults, once they have broken, moult fairly quickly and at times really heavily. In my rabbit operation this is the time breeding stops and my efforts are concentrated on moulting the rabbits as quickly as possible. Special attention given to these rabbits, particularly the bucks, can pay dividends later. Most importantly, I disturb these rabbits as little as possible, they are only handled when being cleaned out or for the weekly health check.

Every day I remove all loose hair in the cage, also hay not eaten from the previous day.

Each rabbit is treated differently, if they like a particular food I see that they get it. Some rabbits go off their food when moulting so I encourage them all to eat. Oily foods are good for moulting rabbits but should only be given in small quantities, as titbits, e.g. a few peanuts and sunflower seeds. In recent years I have given a touch of hemp seed and niger seed from my birdroom and the rabbits relish it. Only a few hemp seeds are given and I have not come across one rabbit that will not eat it. I have previously given Minadex as a vitamin supplement but now use Entrodex, as mentioned previously, both are very good for ensuring that the appetite remains stable.

To the heavily moulting rabbits I also add Cod Liver Oil to the feed twice each week. As Cod Liver Oil can soon go rancid when mixed with food I only mix enough food with the oil to be used that day.

I do not use green food but for people who wish to do so small amounts of the following will assist rabbits when moulting.

Groundsel is very good, but too much acts as a laxative. Small amounts of Comfrey are also beneficial. This would counteract with the Groundsel as it is an astringent. Some greenfoods are excellent conditioners and can be really useful in the moulting period. Chicory is very good as a coat conditioner and can be grown between April and September, so it is available when rabbits are in full moult.

A rabbit that is off its food can be encouraged to eat by offering a small sprig of Rosebay Willow Herb. I fed green food many years ago but have stopped because some grass verges are sprayed with chemicals to suppress weeds and unfortunately the wind can play its part in polluting wider areas. Also pollution by large industrial areas has become more of a problem. Great care needs to be taken to avoid places where dogs are prone to visit. Growing your own greens is by far the best option.

As mentioned above Chicory is an excellent crop to grow for rabbits, I only grow Spinach for the birds, as my garden is small, and these moult out very well on it. I am sure it would be a good green food for rabbits, but a small crop would have to be grown and for this a larger space would be needed, much more than I have, for a constant fresh supply.

Finally on the subject of moult, it can definitely be said that special attention to feeding will ensure a good quick moult. A glossy coat and sound body condition will always make the judge happy. A fit rabbit in an even class for quality should always take the card.

If a rabbit is eating well but is not in good condition worms could be the cause. Sometimes worms can be seen in the droppings, but not always. In this situation a gentle worming will sort the trouble out. I use Johnson's puppy wormer, just a very mild dose in the drinker. Do not forget that the Dwarf rabbit is small so care should be taken when worming. I never worm a rabbit under four months of age. If the beginner is in doubt about worming perhaps a chat with the vet could be useful. Prescribed wormers such as Panacur are expensive but are gentle and effective.

The rabbit definitely benefits from a regular cleansing of the system. For this reason my stock are not fed one day per week, when I add Vanodine V18 to the drinking water in a very mild solution. Before I used Vanodine I coloured the water with Potassium Permanganate crystals using only enough to slightly colour the water. Both are beneficial to the stock but I prefer Vanodine as it has more uses, especially as a disinfectant.

Heat stroke can have a devastating effect on rabbits and in this situation they can die. This is most likely to happen in a sustained spell of very hot weather. Casualties should be wrapped in a wet towel in an effort to cool them down as quickly as possible. If precautions are taken to ensure the rabbit is kept cool the above would not happen.

A rabbit shed is best sited out of direct sunshine. My own rabbitry is placed in an ideal place and is always cool in summer. It is at the bottom of the garden enclosed by very tall bushes which puts the rabbitry in the shade for most of the day. Only late evening sunshine touches the shed and this does not cause a problem.

The combination of direct sun and poor ventilation can really cause health problems in the rabbitry. If your rabbit shed is in the open it is still possible to make it cooler for the stock. Any windows can be shaded with fine green mesh, used for shading greenhouses and can be obtained from a garden centre. The roof can be painted with solar reflecting paint which really works well as it drastically reduces heat in the shed. On very hot days the outside of the shed can be hosed down occasionally.

Hutch gnawing is a pastime most rabbit's resort to. Sometimes it is boredom, in a lot of cases it is part of the rabbits make-up. An example of this is a doe due to kindle and performing her nesting ritual. A lot of damage can be avoided when hutches are being constructed. The less edges a rabbit can get its teeth into the better. Around door frames is a favourite place for chewing. These can be trimmed with right-angled plastic strips, or the full inside of the door can be totally meshed.

Pieces of fruit tree or willow tree could be placed in the hutch. These should be thoroughly scrubbed in a solution of Vanodine. Perhaps the best option is to make a 'cross' out of softwood, this should be large enough so that it will not get buried in the shavings and prevents the rabbit from throwing it about.

Thorough cleaning of hutches is a sure way of limiting the spread of disease and controlling bacterial build up. It does not matter how often you clean out but it should be done thoroughly when you do.

I clean out my hutches every two or three weeks and the dirty corners more regularly. All cages are thoroughly cleaned of all bedding. The bottom of the cages then get sprayed with a strong solution of Vanodine V18.

From time to time I use other disinfectants. Parvocids is very good. I have recently used Genie by Stock Nutrition, another good product. I prefer Vanodine because of its wider range of uses. I also use it, in a less strong solution, to clean food pots and drinkers etc.

Cleaning of drinkers is especially important when additives such as Entrodex and Minadex are being used. Although they are very good products build up of slime occurs. A regular cleaning of the bottle with a bottle brush removes this and also an occasional sterilizing in Milton. I try to renew drinkers every two or three years, by this time a lot have become very worn especially around the nipple.

Now back to the hutch cleaning. The side walls of the cage are given a quick spray of Dyna-mite solution, this is done in the summer, as an added protection against fleas and lice. The floor of the cage is then covered by a generous amount of white shavings. I never use hardwood shavings as they are hard to the rabbit's feet and can stain the rabbits badly. Also the reaction of some hardwood shavings with urine can emit a deadly toxic gas, which could kill the stock. In extremely cold weather I put a layer of oat or barley straw on top of the shavings. This can be really beneficial to the breeding does especially when litters are due. Cages that house doe and feeding litters or young weaners are cleaned out every few days. This ensures that stale food is not picked up by the youngsters.

Fly control is very important in the summer as disease can be brought into the rabbitry by them. The fine greenhouse mesh, mentioned earlier, can be placed over any existing mesh or open windows to stop flies entering. I also use Vapona fly strips which are hung from the shed roof. These strips are also effective against fleas, lice and mite. I renew them every Spring as they remain active all the time the fly problem is at its worst. The old-fashioned fly papers are good but do not look very attractive and availability can be a problem. The Dyna-mite solution can also be used to good effect, especially in a very fine spray.

It does not matter which method is used if the flies are kept at bay. In very hot weather inspection of new born litters and the removal of any dead babies can minimise the effect of flies and keep other problems at bay.

Vermin control is also very important to a rabbit's health. This has been discussed before but a little more information can be helpful. I use poison and a live trap. It is better to keep changing the poison from time to time. Mice can become used to a certain brand and not take it as readily. The live trap is very useful when mice are first starting to enter the shed. It is, usually, the buck mouse looking for a potential breeding place that is the first to enter. In his efforts to inspect the premises he sometimes finds himself caught in the live trap. Mice caught live in a trap occasionally attract others, I have often found three or four caught at the same time. This is usually after a period of not seeing any mice. In recent years ultra sound devices have come onto the market, these are set on a high frequency to affect mice only. Unlike flies, vermin is a problem all year round. A cosy rabbit shed with plenty of hay and food provide mice with an excellent winter retreat, so be on guard at all times.

Your dwarf's claws will need to be cut on a regular basis. I have a set pattern of cutting claws as follows. At around the six months stage nearly all rabbits will need to have their claws cut.

Bucks with potential show careers have a pedicure at this age and are checked on a regular basis throughout their showlife. The only time I do not cut their claws is when they are heavily moulting, it is better to wait until they are finished. There is nothing worse for a judge to handle an otherwise good rabbit, only to find that its claws need cutting. This can affect the rabbit's placing and usually keeps it out of the challenges.

Does are treated differently, after the initial cut the claws are inspected prior to being mated. Over long claws can damage baby rabbits, so if you cut the mother's claws before mating you will never experience this. With maiden does of less than six months old that are ready for mating, cut just the tips of the claws. Following the above method there is never a time when any rabbit's claws are over-length.

Cutting claws can be a difficult operation for a beginner. If the rabbit has been well handled the task will be easier, so this is the first priority. Clippers come in all shapes and sizes, a good quality pair will last for years.

I like to sit down to cut claws so adopt the following method. In a sitting position the rabbit is placed on my lap, facing me. I have the clippers at the right hand side of me as I gently groom the rabbit before taking them up. I hold the rabbit's head in my left hand with my thumb under its chin. With the rabbit's back feet firmly in my lap, I gently ease the head back and this puts the front feet in a good position for cutting. There are five claws to be cut on each front foot. The difficult part is locating each claw, whilst still holding the clippers, with practice this becomes easier. With the rabbit's back feet firmly in your lap there is less chance of the rabbit kicking. If it does try to move or kick a little slight pressure applied with the thumb under the chin has the effect of stopping it. To cut the back claws tip the rabbit further onto its back. With practice, one foot can be left firmly in your lap whilst the other is being cut.

Perhaps for the first few times the beginner might be better assisted by someone more experienced, or at least have someone to hold a foot etc. Follow a method, such as above, claw cutting should become easier and take only a couple of minutes.

Great care must be taken not to cut into the part of the claw where there is a blood supply. This especially so in a dark coloured rabbit as this is more difficult to see. Gentle pressure on the toe just above the claw will show where the blood supply finishes. For the first few times of cutting it is best to keep well away from this point. I always have at hand a solution of Vanodine in a small container, so that if I do cut a claw and it bleeds I dip the foot in the solution to avoid infection.

My final point is, ringing the rabbit's leg. This is best done with Dwarfs between the ages of six and eight weeks. If left until later than this there could be difficulty with the ring going over the hock joint. Also ringing later can cause the rabbit to be distressed or to resent the ring and cause it to bite it, therefore damaging the ring and maybe the rabbit's leg also.

Ringing is sometimes an easier task with the help of an assistant. The rabbit's leg needs to be fully extended so that the ring can be slid easily over the hock joint. One person could hold the rabbit and extend the leg whilst the assistant does the ringing. It is important that the rabbit is held firmly and not allowed to kick during the ringing operation.

The way I ring a rabbit on my own is to place its head under my left arm, securing the back end of the rabbit with my left hand. The leg can then be extended with the right hand and the ring quickly slipped on. I would advise the beginner to see this done by an experienced breeder before attempting it themselves. It is much better to use the assistant and avoid hurting the rabbit.

All the rabbits in my stud that have either breeding or show potential are rung. Ringing is a must for record purposes; I try not to ring pets however. The new owner on seeing the ring could think he had a pedigree dwarf and this could lead to inferior stock being used for breeding and perhaps poor stock reaching the show bench.

This sometimes happens when some newcomers start to breed Dwarfs, although all is not lost as quality can be improved as the fancier gets more into the hobby.

There are definitely more problems that the beginner breeder will come across but some of the preventative methods outlined above could sort quite a few problems out.

After thirty years of breeding Dwarfs I am still experiencing new problems that all add to the challenge of breeding the dwarf rabbit.

CHAPTER 12

Dwarfing Down & Creating New Colours

THE CHALLENGE to create something new will always appeal to a minority of people who are involved in breeding small livestock. The Netherland Dwarf rabbit has all the ingredients necessary to satisfy this appeal.

When the standard was changed to accept any colour, as long as it follows the normal pattern of other breeds, I thought the flood gates would have opened for many new colours reaching the show bench.

This has not been the case and illustrates just how difficult it is to get a new colour established with dwarf characteristics.

In the late sixties I had a little experience of trying to dwarf down a colour. At the time I had a successful stud of New Zealand Reds. The idea of a Red Netherland Dwarf appealed to me, so I gave it a try. Not many people know of my efforts. The standard at that time did not accept such a colour and my idea was to breed a red dwarf and suddenly to appear with it at a national stock show and exhibit it in the unstandardised class. This was never to be and the nearest I got to enjoying a red dwarf was the television series of the same name.

With all practical experience in livestock breeding there is always something to be learned. In the remainder of this chapter I will try to explain where I went wrong, hopefully this will avoid the same mistakes being made by other people. As the book is, basically, about breeding dwarfs with the beginner in mind, I will explain how, as a one time beginner myself, went wrong.

Although I knew the New Zealand Reds pretty well I had bred dwarfs for only three years and did not know enough about them to sort out the problems that occurred.

The beginner breeder should really get used to successfully breeding dwarfs in the easier colours before progressing to dwarfing down a colour from another breed. Having said that, if someone has a passion for starting a dwarfing down project it might be best to start whilst the interest is there. Much dedication will be required, also patience. If you are a fancier who wishes to show every week, such a project is not for you.

Before starting on any dwarfing down it is best to learn as much as possible about the breed of the colour to be dwarfed down. Some breeds have certain peculiarities where colour is concerned so it is wise to know as much as possible. Try asking the person you acquired your stock from for information concerning the breed.

The basic principle of the programme is as follows:

The buck is the mainstay of the operation and should be a good typed Netherland Dwarf as near to the standard as possible. The doe should be a good example of the chosen breed, especially where colour is concerned.

The main objective is to fix the Netherland Dwarf type on the colour chosen. To do this we have to linebreed the doe to the Netherland dwarf buck. Youngsters from the initial pairing will be F1 and the best doe for colour from these needs to be taken back to the original buck to produce F2.

Following the same procedure will give the next generation F3. Once this stage has been reached the F3 should resemble dwarf rabbits with, hopefully, examples being produced with the required colour. This is the basic way to start a breeding programme.

Before giving more details it is important to stress that following the above principle there will be a lot of rabbits bred that will be of no further use in the operation. This is where an outlet for unwanted stock is useful, i.e. the pet shop. As the rabbits are small they are usually acceptable as pets. At the time I was working on the reds I bred and raced whippets and boiled rabbit became part of their diet and it certainly improved their stamina and fitness.

Now let us look at the operation in more detail. First the buck. I have mentioned that he should be a good dwarf for type and best you can get. It is also best if he is small, as dwarfing down is the first major obstacle. He should be as near to the colour as possible to the rabbit you are dwarfing down. If you cannot get a near colour at least try to use one that is compatible.

With reds I chose the Agouti which was a big mistake. Too many blacks were bred in the first two generations, so a lot of time was wasted. The best colour to use would have been a good coloured orange or a red Agouti. The latter is very popular in Holland and resembles the Belgian Hare colour.

It is very important that the dwarf buck carries the mutation gene for dwarfism, i.e. Dw Dw. This can be tested by mating to other dwarfs. When lethal babies are being born, to at least two does, he can be presumed to be a carrier of the gene. The reason that this is important is because, when does are line bred to this buck there will be a good chance that a percentage of rabbits bred will have the required Dw dw combination of the dwarf gene which will give us more show type dwarfs. These rabbits carry the true dwarf characteristics so the sooner they appear the better.

I was totally ignorant of these facts when dwarfing the reds.

The final point, where the buck is concerned, is age. The buck has to be young enough to produce three generations. My Agouti buck went sterile at the F2 stage, so another buck had to be used. By having to use a second buck it becomes harder to fix type. This is more so if the original buck was a good example and a Dw Dw carrier. In these situations time is wasted and the patience can wear thin.

Now to the doe. In all cases she will be larger than the dwarf rabbit. As well as possessing good colour it is best to use the smallest doe possible, but runts should be avoided. Getting the two rabbits to mate successfully to produce the F1 generation can be a very comical affair. If the doe is in really good breeding condition, she usually lifts too high for a buck to successfully mate her. In this situation is it best to hold the doe down or place the buck on a custom made platform and hold the doe in place for him. It is advisable to do plenty of repeat matings to make sure the doe has caught.

My advice is to use two unrelated does and line breed each to the buck therefore giving two lines. The reason for this is, although hybrid vigour is present for the first two generations, by the time each line is producing F3's these rabbits can be crossed over and less inbreeding will be involved. Also, the second doe is an insurance policy should the first doe fail to come up with the rabbits required to progress.

Please bear in mind that with using two does there will be a large quantity of rabbits bred that will be of no further use in the operation. Progress depends on the amount of hutch space available for the programme. I would say that a minimum of twelve hutches will be needed for the full breeding programme.

When reasonable rabbits start to appear, selection is the main criteria.

This strict selection needs to be started from the F2 generation onwards. It is no good having the correct colour and poor type or vice-versa.

The next step is to concentrate on breeding the F3's together. If two lines have been taken back to the original buck this will be alright. If only one line has been taken the F3's will be brother and sister. In this situation an F2 rabbit to an F3 rabbit might be the best way to progress.

The second alternative is not as good as the first but sometimes space and bad luck forces the F2 x F3 mating. Does bred from this pairing are better taken back to the original buck. This has a tendency to fix type better but loss of colour could occur and needs watching closely.

The main objective from now on is to breed a good type buck with the best colour possible. This will become your **PRIMARY** stud buck and line breeding the best coloured does should see further improvement. Eventually an outcross will be needed. The best choice would be a close relative of the original buck. This would limit the chance of recessive faults being bred into your new colour strain of dwarfs.

This will now be the ideal time to take proper interest in the colour. The effect of widening the gene pool will be good for the new colour and there will be a better chance of more stock reaching the show bench.

Getting stock on the show scene is a real opportunity for the colour to progress further still. Well! What happened to the red dwarfs?

My progress, or lack of it, came to a stop by outside influences. My rented allotment at the time was sold by the land owner to a building contractor. As I then lived in a terraced house a small 8' x 6' shed was the only space I had. This was used to house a few rapidly improving sable dwarfs. The only other livestock I kept was a faithful blue whippet bitch called Silver. All the other livestock was sold off, the list being as follows: New Zealand Reds Normal, Chinchilla rabbits plus a few various coloured dwarfs including the red dwarfs?, seven whippets, a small stud of racing pigeons, fifty white Leghorn laying hens, four pens of Rhode Island Red Bantams, a few Silky Bantams used for brooding, two trios of Golden Pheasants and a planted aviary containing British birds and canaries, not to mention the goat! There were two large greenhouses and a large vegetable plot. The services of two pensioners who voluntarily helped me were no longer required.

One pensioner looked after the dogs and pigeons and did the training etc. and the other looked after the greenhouses and gardening side. He also helped with the poultry feeding.

It was the end of a livestock era for me which had spanned ten years. Countless happy hours had been spent on the allotment, especially enjoyable after dark hours working down the coal mines.

And the red dwarfs? After four years of working on the project a few misfit colours and four poor-typed mealy coloured dwarfs were the results of my endeavours and these ended up in the freezer along with a few unsold rabbits. Silver had luxury food for quite a few weeks.

Well, enough of the past, now to a success story of creating new colours. The English Marked Dwarf appeared on the scene in the 1980's after much hard work by a well known East Anglian dwarf fancier. In the last few years there has been a revival of interest amongst dwarf fanciers with this new colour. This is one of the most difficult colours to dwarf, even so interest is growing all the time. With the dedication being applied sooner or later more will reach the show bench and be more popular still.

Perhaps this success story will encourage some dwarf fanciers to create more rare colours. It is certainly a challenge worth considering, in fact in my opinion, it is the ultimate challenge of breeding Netherland Dwarfs.

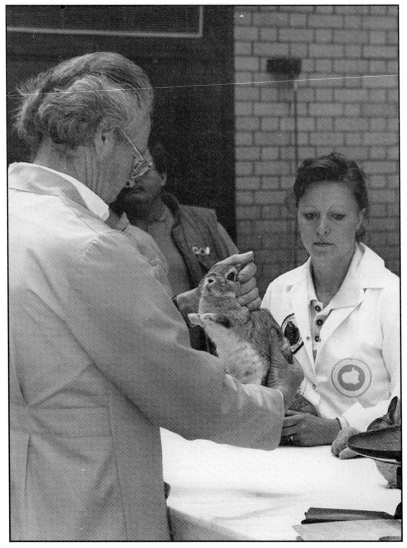

Dennis Pizzey showing the correct way to inspect the underside of a Dwarf.
The left hand goes round the muzzle placing less stress on the ears.
(Taken at the Southern Championship Show)

CHAPTER 13

Judging

TO BE ELECTED TO JUDGE is possibly the highest and most important accolade to bestow on the rabbit fancier. From decisions made at the judging tables top studs are fashioned, the continued success of which depends on good judging. Fanciers climbing the ladder can also rely on the judges' decisions when starting to build their studs and if take their advice, will make successful progress.

We will always need the skill of the judges to compare exhibits to the standard of perfection for each breed. We should realise that judges interpret the standard in different ways. This makes for a healthy fancy, especially in dwarfs. If the same rabbits kept winning the Fancy would become boring.

Even with the slight differences of opinion the really top exhibits seem to win under the majority of judges.

From the above it is easy to see that good quality judging plays a vitally important part in the prestige of the exhibition rabbit fancy. In the Dwarf fancy we have some very good judges but there is always room for potential new judges to climb through the ranks and progress to judging at the highest level.

If the beginner breeder would like to progress to judging, providing the right steps are taken and a positive attitude is adopted, moving up to becoming a judge should be a natural process.

In the rest of this chapter we will go through the steps required to reach judging status, finishing with actual judging.

I must stress that these are strictly my own opinions, so they should be accepted in this context.

The first step the would-be judge should take is to try to build up a moderately successful stud. This is usually a slow process but at first winners can be bought to get you going.

The first real part of the learning process is to start to breed your own winners. By regularly showing good dwarfs and getting placed in the cards you are on your way.

This is the stage where most dwarf breeders show frequently and cover a wide area of shows. It is important to get your name established:

if you are winning with own-bred rabbits, all the better. By building a good stud of dwarfs you will be on the first step of the ladder.

Whilst this is going on, with plenty of shows being attended, the next step can be taken. Stewarding.

When exhibiting at a show ask the show secretary to consider you for stewarding on the dwarf table. Initially all that is needed is a white coat, then watch and learn what the other stewards are doing.

Try to treat every rabbit as though it was your own. The book steward will give you a number of an exhibit. You are then required to remove the rabbit carefully from the pen and place it on the judging table.

Always ensure that the exhibit is correctly labelled and then steady the rabbit down. The judge is always impressed by a good steward so if you handle every rabbit consistently he will be pleased.

Some judges are prepared to talk to stewards and will answer questions whilst judging. Others like to be quiet and concentrate on the task.

Always fall in line with the way the judge wants to work. A good book steward will tell you what is required but with common sense stewarding can become an easy task.

It is better to steward with as many judges as possible. All have different methods and there is much to be learned.

Once you are more experienced in stewarding much more knowledge should have been picked up about the dwarf rabbit. Stewarding at a major stock show is a must. Sometimes only fine points separate the rabbits and you will be on hand to see exactly what goes on.

After stewarding for around twelve months to two years watch the book steward very closely. This is the next step.

Book stewarding for the first time can prove to be difficult but most judges are pleased to help. Usually, after a short time it will be easy to grasp what is required and it becomes very enjoyable. Probably the best time to start is at a show with not many entries and to work for a judge that you know well.

Working at a judging table should be an enjoyable experience and at most shows takes place in a friendly, relaxed atmosphere. When book stewarding you are working really close to the judge. This provides the opportunity of learning more about the dwarf rabbit. Once you have become really efficient at the job, work for as many judges as you can.

At this stage you are almost ready to take the plunge and have a go at being a judge.

It is better to be patient and wait until you are approached by an official of a dwarf club who is keen to put your name forward to be elected to the judging panel. Once nominated your name will be placed on the ballot for election of officers and judges.

There are two ways to be elected to the National Dwarf panel of judges. The first is to be elected to the National panel itself. Nominations are required to be with the secretary the previous June to be placed on the ballot sheet for the following year.

Each fully paid up member receives a ballot sheet, the resulting top forty judges that are elected provide the panel for that particular year. Sometimes it is difficult to be elected to the National panel the first time. If judging is for you do not give up, seek nomination the following year.

The second way to become a National judge is through your regional club's ballot. This is sometimes the easiest way, especially if your name is not well known throughout the country.

The top two judges on the ballot are nominated to the National panel each year. By being on the regional ballot you can qualify to be one of their judges. So, if you have missed out on qualifying for the National panel, your judging career could still be started.

On being elected to the judges panel it could be quite a while until your first engagement. This time should be used well. My advice would be to study the Dwarf Standard well, particularly the requirements for all the different colours. Look for an opportunity to judge a junior section. Practical hands-on knowledge can be learned from such an experience.

When I first started judging, informal and friendly box shows were all the rage. When judging was finished the old fanciers would point out where you went wrong.

There was nothing to beat this practical experience and the tuition received. I have never believed in judging examinations, I think that practical guidance from our most experienced judges could be utilised to the overall improvement of standards of judging.

Now, let us look at judging itself.

When I first started judging I was taught two things. First of all, enjoy what you are doing.

Personally I still find judging to be the most enjoyable part of the hobby. My advice to anyone who does not enjoy judging would be to pack it in, it is not for you.

The second teaching was, to observe the unwritten rule 'Judge's decision is final'. I have always followed this rule as an exhibitor, so I expect the same from fanciers when I am judging.

Constructive criticism should always be welcomed by the judge but his final decision should be respected.

It is always a good idea to arrive at the venue early for a judging engagement. This helps to get the feel of the occasion.

Most judges get a little nervous before actually starting to judge. Even after many years of judging I still get a feeling that would be hard to explain. It is a kind of nervous excitement but this soon goes when the rabbits are handled.

I feel it is really important to have a good book steward. If the paperwork is well under control and the stewards are working well, full concentration can be given to the rabbits.

Before judging commences it is best to ensure that all rabbits are present for that class, also that they are the right colour.

Rabbits that are left in the pen can be very disappointing to the exhibitor and it is so easy for the judge to be blamed. When a rabbit comes to the table and is the wrong colour for the class, it could be sent back and not judged. In this situation I always send the book steward to the secretary and let them sort it out. After all, it could be someone who is showing for the first time and thus could result in disappointment.

It is a must that each rabbit is handled consistently, by following a set pattern.

First, I look for disqualification points. If a rabbit is carrying a disqualification it is pointless assessing it any further and it is sent back to the pen. A note is placed next to the exhibit on the judging slip with the exact reason for disqualification.

Although the standard of perfection is set out by allocating points to each section, judging in the U.K. is usually done by comparison. When judging I use two methods simultaneously. One is a fault analysis and the other is a quality assessment.

As well as these two methods I have the breakdown of points for each section of the standard firmly fixed in my mind. It may sound complicated but it isn't.

Each exhibit is handled as follows:

Once I am satisfied it hasn't any disqualification points, an overall look of the exhibit is made. A mental note is made of any fault it is carrying. The exhibit is then placed at the top of the line for the time being.

The next exhibit is then assessed in exactly the same way. If it has less faults than the first it goes above it. This is the fault analysis part of the judging operation.

If a rabbit comes to hand that is hard to fault, quality assessment comes into play. If it is good I spend a bit of time with it. These exhibits are the judges' friend and its qualities will take it to the top of the table. This rabbit becomes the yardstick by which the rest of the class is judged.

My next objective is to, hopefully, find a rabbit as good, if not better, than it. Rabbits that come to hand with a few faults again are placed in line accordingly. This process is carried out until all exhibits have been seen.

In a class of two or three exhibits they are quickly checked again before the final placings are made. There is always a possibility of taking too much time with exhibits, or at the other end of the scale, being too quick and missing something.

The important thing is to master the art of giving every exhibit a reasonable amount of time to show off its qualities. If I have difficulty splitting two rabbits the breakdown of the standard of points comes into the equation.

Whilst handling both rabbits in turn, I mentally go through the standard of points for each feature. The rabbit scoring the highest points gets the placing.

If this is happening at the top end of the table, extra care is taken. In the eventuality that they are both still equal the one nearer to the ideal weight gets the ticket.

With combination of fault analysis, quality assessment and, if need be, the break down of standard points the best balanced rabbit to the standard will have been found.

This balance is really important because it isn't any good if the exhibit excels in one feature only. When I am judging, overall balance is my main priority when selecting winners. This is especially so when placing the exhibit for best of breed.

Once I have my winner and the ring number is taken, it gets another quick assessment. This serves two purposes. First, a quick mental note can be made of its good qualities, knowing that I am going to handle it again.

If I do this after every class I usually have a rough mental picture where the rabbit will be placed in the mixed duplicate classes. Getting proficient with this particular aspect usually ensures that the duplicate classes can be sorted with little fuss.

In the event that two rabbits are very close in a class, both are considered for the duplicate classes. The second rabbit in a particular class could be good enough to beat the actual winner of another class later on in the proceedings.

The rabbits that are close should be noted in your critique, which is the second reason for the quick assessment on completing the class.

It is sometimes difficult to put what you see into words. It is very important to become proficient with this part of the judging procedure. I usually try to write something good and, also, note the main faults.

An example would be as follows: "good body type and colour, slight fault to ears". Most rabbit fanciers like to see the critique in show reports, so it is vitally important to master the art of show reporting.

I usually write up my show reports within the first two days of the show. The top rabbits are still fresh in my mind and by quickly posting off after completion I catch the publication date of the Fancy's magazine *Fur & Feather*.

To see "no report received" in *Fur & Feather* does not give the judge concerned much credibility.

Well, let us get back to judging. Once all the straight classes have been judged my thoughts turn to Best in Section.

I have always found duplicate judging a fairly easy task.

After all, the rabbits have been looked at once, so it just means looking at the finer points and placings should come easy.

When the last four rabbits are left on the table only minor faults usually separate. Show condition and general well being usually come into play to decide the actual winner.

Foremost in my mind at this time is that the eventual winner will have to be looked at again for possible best in show, so it is really important to select the best and fittest rabbit.

Before I reach this stage, it is important to ensure all duplicate classes are judged and slips signed accordingly. I have a simple method to ensure that this is done without much fuss.

I firmly believe that we have too many duplicate classes at our shows. Even so, as judges we are employed to judge the schedule whatever it is. I usually bring out as many rabbits as possible in the challenge class. These rabbits are placed from one to whatever the number I see fit to be on the table.

The positions are written horizontally on my judging sheet. This then becomes the master from which all duplicate classes are made out. By adopting this method I do not cross myself and life is easier for the book steward. The young classes can be done in the same way, by placing on the next line on the judging sheet. Comparing adult and youngsters together can give us placings for any age classes.

Once all slips are signed along with best of breed and challenge certificates our section is complete.

The next part of the proceedings can be either pleasant or totally frustrating. I refer to joint judging. The idea is to find the best fancy rabbit by utilising the other judges and your consensus of opinion.

Judges experiencing this for the first time can be totally put off the idea of judging rabbits. It is best to study as much as possible the standards of other breeds. If you have judged some junior sections and actually placed other breeds, joint judging will be easier.

Please have faith in the fact that not one judge knows everything about every breed of rabbit. If joint judging with a senior judge it is usually easier. I always try to learn something from these joint judging experiences. It is best to approach the task with an open mind and try to honestly find the best rabbit on the day. The more engagements the new judge has the better joint judging becomes.

It is after judging the first show that a decision should be made about carrying on. It is a long climb up the ladder to the top of the panel. If you enjoy judging it is definitely worth it.

Quick Reference